Offshoring

About the series

The McKinsey Global Institute (MGI) was established in 1990 as an independent economics think tank within McKinsey & Company, the management consultancy, to conduct original research on critical economic issues. Its primary purpose is to provide insights and facts about developments in the global economy that will help business leaders and policymakers to make better decisions.

This anthology of articles published by MGI is part of a multi-volume set. Each volume presents conclusions drawn from MGI's principal research projects, in particular over the past five years, illuminating related themes.

The Productivity Imperative: Wealth and Poverty in the Global Economy

Articles in this volume show why and how the level of productivity in an economy—the ratio of output to input—is the key determinant of its rate of growth. In studies of numerous economies around the world, both developed and emerging, MGI has measured productivity levels sector by sector and analysed how they might be improved.

Driving Growth: Breaking Down
Barriers to Global Prosperity

This series book describes three barriers to productivity improvement that MGI has frequently encountered in its studies on productivity in individual countries.

Offshoring: Understanding
the Emerging Global Labor Market

This volume in this series of anthologies contains articles that estimate the likely extent of offshoring and how businesses and policymakers on both sides of this emerging global labor market can better manage the phenomenon. The key is not to obstruct offshoring, but instead to make sure that some of the resulting gains are directed towards those who lose out from it.

Offshoring

Understanding the
Emerging Global Labor Market

Edited by Diana Farrell,
McKinsey Global Institute

Harvard Business School Press
Boston, Massachusetts

Copyright 2006 McKinsey & Company, Inc. United States

Printed in the United States of America

10 09 08 07 06   5 4 3 2 1

ISBN 10: 1-4221-1007-9
ISBN 13: 978-1-4221-1007-2

Library of Congress Cataloging-in-Publication Data is forthcoming.

The paper used in this publication meets the minimum requirements of the
American National Standard for Information Sciences—Permanence of
Paper for Printed Library Materials, ANSI Z39.48-1992.

Contents

Understanding offshoring

Offshoring is contentious. Policy makers, business executives, and thought leaders express strong and often conflicting opinions on the growing practice among companies from developed economies of employing college graduates in emerging markets, where labor costs are lower, to carry out service functions previously done at home. As the range of tasks that can be done offshore has expanded to include activities critical to company performance, such as research and new product design, as well as back office and support jobs, so debate has become more heated.

Over the past four years, the McKinsey Global Institute (MGI) has been studying offshoring intensively. Our aim is to give decision makers and shapers in government and business a better understanding of the scope and economics of offshoring as well as its effects, so they can test their opinions against facts, and draw new conclusions. This anthology presents what we consider our most substantial contributions to the offshoring debate.

Offshoring may appear to be a recent trend, but relocating jobs to cut costs is nothing new. Many manufacturing plants in the northeastern United States, for instance, moved to the South and Southwest during the 1980s to save money. Having services performed offshore in other countries is simply a more recent expression of the same corporate impulse.

The ability to offshore depends on there being a pool of well-educated job candidates offshore, a sizable gap between their pay expectations and those of their peers in the employer's home market, robust distributed communications technology, a set of liberal trade rules, and growing confidence among companies in the stability of emerging markets. These conditions have increasingly been met by emerging markets since the mid 1990s. Conditions favored the development of global trade in goods and capital somewhat earlier. In offshoring, we see the development of a similarly global market for labor to carry out those jobs no longer tied to a particular location. MGI's investigation of this emerging global labor market is in line with our mission to inform decision makers about the transition to a global economy.

Offshoring has important implications for companies and countries on both the "demand" and the "supply" sides of the market. At the highest level, it represents an opportunity for multinational companies to create more value at lower cost. As such, it means a boost in productivity for the global economy. Put another way, it helps to create a bigger cake for the world's population to share. But gains from offshoring do not automatically flow to all the people it affects, notably those workers in developed economies who are displaced as a result. And although offshoring will result in a net increase in employment worldwide, the practice means that individual service jobs—in emerging as well as developed markets—feel less secure. Workers perceive their employers may switch location at any time, as relative labor costs shift. Employees in emerging markets may experience a disconcerting gulf between the timetables and expectations of offshore employers and local custom and practice.

In sum, offshoring is an economic phenomenon with significant potential to increase the world's wealth. But it also increases the pace of change in the societies that it affects, placing new strains on them, and presenting their policy makers with complex choices. These all need to be carefully managed if the economic benefits from offshoring are to translate into net social gains in developed and emerging markets. This anthology aims to help decision makers manage offshoring better.

We have included ten of MGI's published articles on the topic, arranged in four sections.

1. Sizing the emerging global labor market

The impact of offshoring on developed countries and emerging markets alike depends on its potential magnitude and the pace at which it develops. "Sizing the emerging global labor market" estimates the global demand for and supply of offshore talent in service occupations such as engineering, accounting, R&D, and generalists. On the demand side, we estimate the proportion of all service jobs that could possibly be performed remotely, how many of those jobs at present are being done in offshore locations, and how that figure is likely to change by 2008. On the supply side, we estimate the total pool of skilled graduates in emerging markets and the fraction of that pool both suitable and available to work for multinational companies, broken down by occupation; and we estimate the future supply of available offshore talent to 2008. The figures show that although offshoring is growing fast, it is a far smaller phenomenon than it could be in theory, and is likely to remain so.

China and India loom large in the global labor market because of their sheer size. So far, India has far outstripped China in attracting offshore jobs. The subcontinent has developed a formidable IT and business-processing sector, with several world-class companies. But even India's supply of graduates is not infinite. In some parts of the country, demand for engineers has already almost caught up with supply, and wages are rising. "Ensuring India's offshoring future" recommends policy changes needed in India to ensure that this new global market, already an important source of growth, will be an equally important contributor to India's prosperity in years to come. "China's looming talent shortage" shows how China's supply of skilled graduates suitable for professional services work in multinational companies, though immense, will not be large enough to satisfy demand from either foreign or domestic companies in China unless policy makers can implement far-reaching changes in the country's education system.

2. Putting offshoring in context

The offshoring trend evokes enormous political controversy in both developed economies, where it may displace workers, and in emerging markets, where policy makers worry about foreign companies crowding out incumbents and exploiting workers. Policy makers in both sets of countries have thus called for measures to stop offshoring or to limit its reach.

This would be a mistake. "Who wins in offshoring?" demonstrates how offshoring creates wealth for the US economy as a whole, even if some workers lose their jobs.

From the perspective of emerging markets, offshoring is just a new variant of foreign direct investment (FDI). As such, our research shows that it will be to their overall economic benefit, even if some incumbent domestic companies lose market share. "The truth about foreign direct investment in emerging markets" describes the research from which we draw this conclusion. Examining the effects of FDI on both service and manufacturing industries in Brazil, China, India, and Mexico, MGI has found overwhelmingly that it raises local standards of living and creates good jobs. Moreover, local graduates employed by offshoring companies often go on to start their own; many of the executives working for India's offshoring giants today started their careers with foreign companies.

3. Capturing the offshore opportunity

How and where to offshore are critical strategic decisions facing top management in medium to large companies today. The potential gains may be immense, but there is equal scope for making expensive mistakes.

At present, most companies are doing more or less the same things offshore that they have been doing at home, in the same fashion but at lower cost. However, the difference in the labor to capital cost ratio in emerging markets means that redesigned offshore processes could be much more productive. "Offshoring and beyond" examines these opportunities.

So far, companies setting up in offshore locations have tended to choose cities where other companies have gone before. As a result, some offshore "magnets" like Prague and Bangalore are already suffering a labor squeeze and rapidly rising wages, even though supplies of skilled labor in emerging markets as a whole are plentiful. "Smarter offshoring" recommends to companies an analytical approach to selecting the optimal place to offshore. When companies choose more carefully, demand for offshore talent will spread more evenly across the many emerging markets where supplies are deep, and companies will lock in their advantage from offshoring for longer.

4. Rethinking the policy response

Section four looks at the policy options that offshoring presents to political leaders in developed economies, and recommends choices. MGI's research has shown that the net gain to the US economy from offshoring is unequivocal. Yet there are calls for curbs on offshoring from the United States, because of fears of its impact on the domestic job market. "US offshoring: rethinking the response" shows why regulating against offshoring would be a mistake. Instead, the government and corporations should use some of their gains from offshoring to help offset the hardship of those who do lose their jobs as a result, and to prepare the workforce generally for the faster rate of job change that goes with more open, global competition.

European economies are prominent among the new offshore employers, yet many of them have a different challenge. Our research shows that the French and German economies will lose out from the offshoring trend unless they adjust their domestic policies to encourage faster reemployment of workers. Their offshoring companies are loath to invest resulting gains in job-creating ventures at home, where labor market regulations make hiring workers very costly. "How France and Germany can benefit from offshoring" explains how changing labor market policy to make it more attractive for companies to employ workers at home could turn that loss around, enabling them to receive the net economic benefit that the US enjoys.

"Governing globalization," our concluding essay, urges companies and governments alike to do more to help those workers who are adversely affected by offshoring, especially by aiding them to make the transition into new employment.

Offshoring represents a new global market in labor made possible by today's technologies and greater integration between emerging and developed economies. It can have both positive and negative effects. But if decision makers understand the phenomenon and manage it well, we believe the impact of offshoring can be broadly positive for all societies that engage in it.

—Diana Farrell
Director, McKinsey Global Institute

1

Sizing the emerging global labor market

**Diana Farrell, Martha A. Laboissière,
and Jaeson Rosenfeld**

IDEAS IN BRIEF

Reductions in the cost of global telecommunications are producing what amounts to a single market for jobs that can be performed remotely.

Today that global market is small. But as it grows, the demand for offshore labor from the developed world's companies will increasingly affect wage rates and employment levels in the developing world.

Offshoring is unlikely to create any sudden discontinuities in overall levels of employment and wages in developed countries.

Both companies and countries can take specific measures to help clear supply and demand more efficiently in this nascent global market.

The topic of offshoring generates extreme differences of opinion among policy makers, business executives, and thought leaders. Some have argued that nearly all service jobs will eventually move from developed economies to low-wage ones.[1] Others say that rising wages in cities such as Bangalore and Prague indicate that the supply of offshore talent is already running thin.[2]

To a large extent, these disagreements reflect the confusion surrounding the newly integrating and still inefficient global labor market. Much as technology change is making it possible to integrate global capital markets into a single market for savings and investment, so digital communications are giving rise to what is, in effect, a single global market for those jobs that can now, thanks to IT, be performed remotely from customers and colleagues.

The newly integrating nature of this global labor market has strategic and tactical implications for companies and countries alike. Information and insight about it are sparse, however, and executives and policy makers have little of either for making the decisions they face. To provide help for governments and companies in both high- and low-wage economies, the McKinsey Global Institute (MGI) analyzed the potential availability of offshore talent in 28 low-wage nations and the likely demand for it in service jobs across eight of the developed world's sectors (chosen as a representative cross-section of the global economy): automotive (service jobs only), financial services, health care, insurance, IT services, packaged software, pharmaceuticals (service jobs only), and retailing. These sectors provide about 23 percent of the nonagricultural jobs in developed countries. The study,[3] which projects trends to 2008, aims to assess the dynamics of supply and demand for offshore service talent at the occupational, sectoral, and global level and thus the likely impact on both employment and wages in the years ahead.[4]

MGI's analysis provides a panoramic view of the offshoring of services, as well as a number of useful conclusions, including:

- Offshoring will probably continue to create a relatively small global labor market—one that threatens no sudden discontinuities in overall levels of employment and wages in developed countries.

- Demand for offshore labor by companies in the developed world will increasingly push up wage rates for some occupations in low-wage countries, but not as high as current wage levels for those occupations in developed ones.

- Potential global supply and likely demand for offshore talent are matched inefficiently, with demand outstripping supply in some locations and supply outstripping demand in others.

The more efficiently the emerging global labor market functions, of course, the more value it will create for its participants by allocating resources more economically. Both companies and countries can take specific measures to raise its efficiency in clearing demand and supply.

The demand for offshore talent

Broadly speaking, a suitably qualified person anywhere in the world could undertake any task that requires neither substantial local knowledge nor physical or complex interaction between an employee and customers or colleagues. Using these criteria, we estimate that 11 percent of service jobs around the world could be carried out remotely.

Of course, some sectors provide an unusually large number of such jobs. As a rule, industries with more customer-facing functions have less potential in this respect. Consequently, the retailing sector, in which the vast majority of employees work in stores, could offshore only 3 percent of its jobs by 2008. Yet because retailing is such a huge employer around the world, this would be equivalent to 4.9 million positions. In contrast, by 2008 it will be possible to undertake remotely almost half of all jobs in the packaged-software industry, but in this far less labor-intensive business, that represents only 340,000 positions.

Some occupations also are more amenable than others to remote employment. The most amenable to it are engineering, on the one hand, and finance and accounting, on the other (52 percent and 31 percent, respectively). The work of generalist and support staff is much less amenable (9 percent and 3 percent, respectively), because those workers interact with their customers or colleagues extensively. But generalists and support workers permeate every industry and therefore provide the highest absolute number of jobs that remote talent could fill: a total of 26 million.

In practice, just a small fraction of the jobs that could go offshore actually will. Today, around 565,000 service jobs in the eight sectors we evaluated have been offshored to low-wage countries. By 2008, that number will grow to 1.2 million. Extrapolating these numbers to the entire global economy, we estimate that total offshore employment will grow from 1.5 million jobs in 2003 to 4.1 million in 2008—just 1 percent of the total number of service jobs in developed countries. To put this number in perspective (in what is, to be sure, not a direct comparison), consider the fact that an average of 4.6 million people in the United States started work with new employers every month in the year ending March 2005.[5]

Why is the gap between the potential and actual number of jobs moving offshore so large? Many observers think that regulatory barriers stand in the way, but MGI interviews indicate that company-specific considerations (such as management attitudes, organizational structure, and scale) are generally more powerful deterrents.[6] Companies cite cost pressures as the main incentive to hire offshore labor, for example, but the strength of cost pressures varies by sector. Many companies lack sufficient scale to justify the costs of offshoring. Others find that the functions they could offshore in theory must actually stay where they are because their internal processes are so complex. Often, managers are wary of overseeing units on the other side of the world or unwilling to take on the burden of extra travel.

The supply of talent in low-wage nations

On the supply side, developing countries produce far fewer graduates suitable for employment by multinational companies than the raw numbers might suggest. Nonetheless, the potential supply of appropriate workers is large and growing fast, and some small countries boast surprisingly large numbers of them.

The 28 low-wage countries we studied have some 33 million young professionals: university graduates with up to seven years of work experience.[7] The eight higher-wage nations in our study have 15 million—7.7 million in the United States alone.

Yet interviews with 83 human-resources managers for multinationals operating in low-wage economies indicate that, on average, only 13 percent of the university graduates from the 28 low-wage nations are suitable for jobs in these companies (see "Fewer than you'd think"). The HR managers give a variety of reasons for the problem, especially a lack of language skills, an emphasis on theory at the expense of practical knowledge, and a lack of cultural fit (meaning interpersonal skills, as well as attitudes toward teamwork and flexible work, that are at odds with the norm in multinationals).[8]

The proportion of suitable job candidates varies by occupation and, even more, by country. So while 50 percent of the engineers in Hungary or Poland, for example, could work for multinational companies, only 10 percent and 25 percent of those in China and India, respectively, could do so. In general,

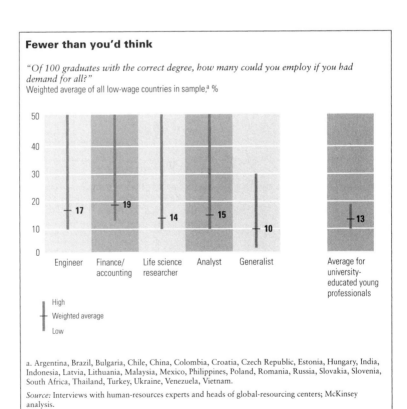

Fewer than you'd think

"Of 100 graduates with the correct degree, how many could you employ if you had demand for all?"
Weighted average of all low-wage countries in sample,[a] %

Engineer — 17
Finance/accounting — 19
Life science researcher — 14
Analyst — 15
Generalist — 10
Average for university-educated young professionals — 13

High
Weighted average
Low

a. Argentina, Brazil, Bulgaria, Chile, China, Colombia, Croatia, Czech Republic, Estonia, Hungary, India, Indonesia, Latvia, Lithuania, Malaysia, Mexico, Philippines, Poland, Romania, Russia, Slovakia, Slovenia, South Africa, Thailand, Turkey, Ukraine, Venezuela, Vietnam.

Source: Interviews with human-resources experts and heads of global-resourcing centers; McKinsey analysis.

university graduates from Central European countries are well suited to work for multinationals. By contrast, job candidates from Russia are well educated but often by universities that fail to give them practical skills, while in India the quality of the educational system—top universities apart—handicaps graduates. A lack of strong English language skills is the most pressing issue for Brazil and China.

In large emerging markets, the pool of suitable talent shrinks further because many university graduates live far from major cities with international airline connections (twin criteria for multinational companies seeking offshore locations) and would rather stay close to home. Only one-third of Russian graduates live in major cities, and few of the others are willing to move. By contrast, nearly half of all Indian students graduate from universities close to major international hubs (such as Bangalore, Delhi, Hyderabad, and Mumbai), and Indians are also the most willing to relocate. In China, multinationals face an additional problem: strong competition from companies serving the domestic market.

These "pool-shrinking" factors mean that of the 33 million potential young professionals in the low-wage markets we studied, only about 3.9 million—12 percent—are both suitable for multinationals and realistically available for hire. In our sample of high-wage countries, by contrast, 8.8 million young professionals meet both conditions (see "A shrinking pool").[9] But 3.9 million is still a deep pool. In some occupations, such as engineering, finance and accounting, and quantitative analysis, that number represents 75 percent or more of the suitable labor in our sample of high-wage countries.

Moreover, the amount of suitable labor in low-wage countries is growing fast. Their university graduates are increasing in number at a yearly rate of 5.5 percent, as compared with just

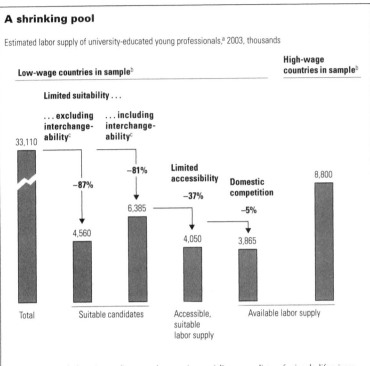

A shrinking pool

Estimated labor supply of university-educated young professionals,[a] 2003, thousands

Low-wage countries in sample[b]

High-wage countries in sample[b]

Limited suitability . . .

. . . excluding interchange-ability[c]

. . . including interchange-ability[c]

33,110

−81%

−87%

6,385

4,560

Limited accessibility

−37%

4,050

Domestic competition

−5%

3,865

8,800

Total

Suitable candidates

Accessible, suitable labor supply

Available labor supply

a. Occupations include engineers, finance and accounting specialists, generalist professionals, life science researchers, and quantitative analysts with ≤7 years of work experience.

b. Low-wage countries: Argentina, Brazil, Bulgaria, Chile, China, Colombia, Croatia, Czech Republic, Estonia, Hungary, India, Indonesia, Latvia, Lithuania, Malaysia, Mexico, Philippines, Poland, Romania, Russia, Slovakia, Slovenia, South Africa, Thailand, Turkey, Ukraine, Venezuela, Vietnam; high-wage countries: Canada, Germany, Ireland, Japan, United Kingdom, and United States; Australia and South Korea studied b y way of extrapolation.

c. For example, unsuitable engineering/life science/finance graduates can still work as quantitative analysts when fulf illing suitability criteria of that group; all unsuitable graduates can still work as generalists when fulfilling suitability criteria of that group.

Source: Government statistics on labor, graduation for countries in sample; interviews with human-resources experts; surveys on student geographical mobility; McKinsey analysis.

1 percent in developed countries. The growth in the ranks of people with qualifications that multinationals actually want is particularly rapid: in just five years, the proportion of degrees awarded in business and economics has jumped to 31 percent of the total, from 18 percent, in Russia and to 36 percent, from 16 percent, in Poland. What's more, by 2008 the supply of suitable young engineers is likely to be almost the same in the developing and developed countries we studied, and suitable finance and

accounting professionals from the developing countries will out-number those from the high-wage ones.

A country's supply of suitable talent, as opposed to its overall number of university graduates, isn't proportional to the size of its population: though China's population is 16 times bigger than that of the Philippines, for instance, its pool of suitable young English-speaking engineers is only three times as big. Poland has nearly as many suitable engineers as does much more populous Russia. The Czech Republic, Hungary, Poland, and Russia together have as many suitable generalists as does India, which has five times their total population, and nearly as many suitable engineers. As a result, many countries besides China and India could play roles in the emerging global labor market.

An imperfect market

In aggregate, the potential supply of offshore talent suitable for employment by multinationals exceeds likely demand in each of the eight occupations[10] we analyzed. In 2008, for instance, the potential supply of support staff and of young professional generalists suitable for employment by multinational companies will exceed likely demand by 98 percent and 78 percent, respectively. Only the potential supply of engineers from low-wage countries looks a little tight at the global level.

But the aggregate view creates an illusion of abundance. In fact, companies that hire offshore talent tend to follow one another to locations with a track record of providing it instead of choosing places that meet each and every need. The concentration of companies does have some positive effects, such as speeding improvements in infrastructure, communications, and the business environment. But eventually that approach can create local imbalances between demand and supply, and these imbalances in turn produce local wage inflation and high levels of attrition among workers.

This kind of concentration is already affecting the supply and cost of labor in some cities in the Czech Republic, India, and Russia. If current demand trends continue, the supply of suitable labor will be squeezed in Prague as early as 2006 and in Hyderabad by 2008, thereby making those cities less attractive for the many companies whose sunk costs in physical and human capital there will make it hard for them to switch locations. If companies were to disperse their demand more widely, overall wage levels for offshore labor would rise more slowly (see "What offshoring may do to wages").

Demand-side implications for companies

Different companies need different things from their offshore locations, depending on their home markets, their primary language, the scale of their plans for offshoring, the decision on whether to outsource or to set up captive operations, and many other factors. Different objectives mean that companies assign different costs and benefits to the same locations—a feature of the global labor market that creates a useful force for dispersing demand and reducing the pressure on wages. But companies must act rationally to control this force by finding better data on the location of suitable talent and then analyzing the real cost of employing it in each of these countries. (See "Choices, choices" for a graphical representation.)

As we have noted, rather than being sidetracked by the absolute number of graduates in a given country, companies

Choices, choices

Strengths and weaknesses of different countries in criteria for offshoring location (from viewpoint of US company), on scale of 1 to 5 where 1 = most attractive, 5 = least attractive

Weighting	50%	10%	10%	10%	10%	10%	
	Cost	Vendor landscape	Domestic market	Risk profile	Business environment	Quality of infrastructure	Location cost index
India	1.5	2.2	3.5	2.7	3.6	3.3	2.3
China	1.8	3.7	1.8	3.4	3.6	2.5	2.4
Malaysia	1.7	4.7	3.3	2.2	3.4	2.5	2.5
Philippines	1.4	4.5	3.5	3.9	3.7	2.8	2.6
Brazil	2.2	3.5	4.2	2.8	3.0	2.0	2.7
Mexico	2.2	4.7	2.8	3.5	2.6	2.0	2.7
Hungary	2.6	4.7	3.3	2.3	2.8	2.8	2.9
Czech Republic	2.6	4.7	3.5	2.2	3.0	3.0	2.9
Poland	2.7	4.0	3.3	2.7	3.1	3.0	3.0
United States	4.4	1.0	2.7	1.7	1.3	1.5	3.0
Canada	3.9	3.2	2.5	1.5	1.7	2.0	3.1
Russia	3.0	4.5	2.8	3.5	3.3	3.3	3.2
United Kingdom	4.6	1.8	2.8	2.1	2.1	2.3	3.4
Germany	4.4	2.5	3.0	1.9	2.5	2.8	3.5
Ireland	4.5	3.5	2.8	1.5	2.5	2.8	3.5
Japan	4.9	2.2	3.0	2.0	3.1	2.3	3.7

● Attractive　● Unattractive

should consider the supply of suitable labor and the demand for it. If they want to gain access to bigger pools of labor and to avoid the negative effects of agglomeration in offshoring hot spots, they should assess a variety of possibilities, including second-tier cities and "telework" options. To work out the specific costs of offshoring in each potential location, companies should define their criteria, which usually include labor costs, the quality of local service vendors, the potential of the local market, its intrinsic risks, the quality of the local infrastructure, and the business environment. Each company can then use its particular goals and requirements to weight the criteria. Once it has gathered such data on all potential locations, it can calculate its true cost of offshoring in any of them and rank them accordingly.

China, India, and the Philippines—the most popular countries for offshoring today—have the lowest average labor costs. They are the most rational choices for companies that rank those costs above anything else. When companies use their vary-

The location cost index

Disguised examples

		Case A	Case B	Case C	Case D
Case profile	Industry	Pharma	Banking	Pharma	Logistics
	Activity	Clinical trial	IT	R&D	IT
	Is company global?	Yes	Yes	Yes	Yes
	Location of headquarters	Europe	United States	United States	Europe
Weighted by	Cost	25	60	25	35
	Vendor landscape	0	20	0	0
	Domestic market	40	0	0	0
	Risk profile	10	5	25	10
	Business environment	10	5	25	30
	Quality of infrastructure	15	10	25	25
Result	Top-ranked countries by model; **company's actual choice**	1. China	1. India	1. United States	1. Hungary
		2. Malaysia	2. China	2. Canada	2. Malaysia
		3. Mexico	3. Philippines	3. Malaysia	**3. Czech Republic**
		4. Canada	4. Malaysia	4. Brazil	4. India

Weighted importance of factor: High ▮▮▮▮▮ Low

Source: Interviews; location cost index database, McKinsey Global Institute.

ing particular needs to rank countries, more locations will emerge as attractive and demand will disperse.

"The location cost index" shows how this dispersion works in practice. Using the location cost index (a data-based tool MGI has developed for companies choosing places to offshore their operations), we ranked countries for four different companies, each with its own criteria for an offshoring location. The results show the diversity of optimal locations, so companies following the herd might be making the wrong choice.

Supply-side implications for countries

Since the demand perspective doesn't beget any general, fixed ranking of offshoring locations, the supply side has no preordained winners and losers. Any country that wants to attract offshoring investments should target the sectors and companies whose needs most closely match what it can already offer and then hone these attractive features. To do so, of course, it must know what they are and which sectors and companies might favor them.

In any case, all supply-side countries would benefit from improving the quality of their talent, not just its quantity. Many developing countries, for example, could make their large potential labor supply more attractive to the multinationals by improving the skills—especially the language skills—of their college graduates. If by 2008 Chinese engineers were as suitable as Indian ones are today, for instance, China's supply of such engineers would nearly double, to 395,000, thereby increasing China's relative attractiveness as an offshoring location. Improving the suitability of graduates is a complex undertaking, but governments can work with domestic and multinational companies to promote training in practical skills at universities and management-training programs.

Governments can also make their countries more attractive to the multinationals in any sector by reducing the level of bureaucratic interference, improving the local infrastructure, increasing the competitiveness of tax regimes, and strengthening intellectual-property laws.

As global labor markets become increasingly integrated, rational action by companies and countries will help facilitate the efficient clearing of supply and demand for jobs.

What offshoring may do to wages

Data about the effects of offshoring on wages are scarce in both the demand- and the supply-side countries. Yet we gained insight into these effects by modeling the outcomes of a variety of hypothetical corporate decisions.

On the supply side

What, for instance, would be the effect on the wages of engineers in emerging markets if labor costs were the most important factor for US companies choosing offshore locations? Our analysis shows that salary levels for engineers in the lowest-cost countries would likely double (see "Wage growth is relative"). But salaries in emerging markets wouldn't reach the prevailing level in the United States or western Europe, since they will be capped at about 30 percent of average US wages, or the current level in Brazil and Mexico.

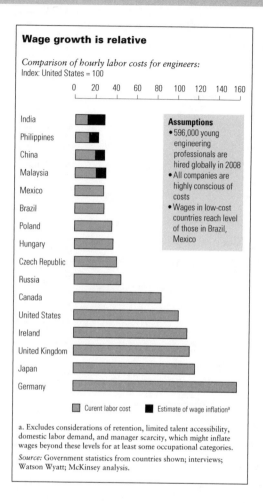

Wage growth is relative

Comparison of hourly labor costs for engineers:
Index: United States = 100

Assumptions
- 596,000 young engineering professionals are hired globally in 2008
- All companies are highly conscious of costs
- Wages in low-cost countries reach level of those in Brazil, Mexico

India
Philippines
China
Malaysia
Mexico
Brazil
Poland
Hungary
Czech Republic
Russia
Canada
United States
Ireland
United Kingdom
Japan
Germany

◻ Current labor cost   ◼ Estimate of wage inflation[a]

a. Excludes considerations of retention, limited talent accessibility, domestic labor demand, and manager scarcity, which might inflate wages beyond these levels for at least some occupational categories.

Source: Government statistics from countries shown; interviews; Watson Wyatt; McKinsey analysis.

Local wage inflation will probably continue in some offshoring locations as long as the multinationals concentrate their demand in a few cities. Because of the sunk costs of setting up an offshore facility, if demand in that location begins to outstrip local supply, the wages paid by individual companies may rise above the levels prevailing in neighboring countries. Dispersing demand will slow down overheating in the hot spots.

Overall, although wages in the supply-side countries will probably rise, they won't reach the level of wages in the demand-side countries.

On the demand side

Companies are moving their operations offshore at a slow pace, which means that over the next five years offshoring will have a negligible effect on overall employment in the demand-side countries for the occupations we analyzed.

Consider the impact in the United States. Over the past 30 years, the share of manufacturing jobs in total US employment has declined by 11 percentage points, to 21 percent, from 32 percent. By comparison, we estimate that only 9 percent of all US service jobs could, even in theory, be performed remotely, and it is unlikely that all of them will move offshore during the next 30 years. Wage levels too are unlikely to drop, for the same reason. Indeed, in the United States, growth rates for wages and the number of jobs in computer and data-processing services—a sector where offshoring is prevalent—are higher than those in the economy as a whole.[a]

This moderate impact and generally slow pace won't soften the blow for people who do lose their employment to offshoring. A sustained effort to retrain them is likely to yield results, since most of them are college graduates.

a. US Bureau of Labor Statistics (SIC 7370: current employment statistics).

The authors wish to thank Charles de Segundo, Robert Pascal, Sascha Stürze, and Fusayo Umezawa for their contributions to the research underlying this article.

Diana Farrell, Martha A. Laboissière, and Jaeson Rosenfeld, *The McKinsey Quarterly, 2005 Number 3.*

Notes

1. Erica Kinetz, "Who wins and who loses as jobs move overseas?" *New York Times,* December 7, 2003.

2. Manjeet Kripalani and Josey Puliyenthuruthel, "India: Good help is hard to find," *BusinessWeek,* February 14, 2005.

3. The full report, *The Emerging Global Labor Market,* is available free of charge at www.mckinsey.com/mgi.

4. The mid- to high-wage countries we studied in depth were Canada, Germany, Ireland, Japan, the United Kingdom, and the United States; Australia and South Korea were studied by way of extrapolation. The low-wage countries studied in depth were Brazil, China, the Czech Republic, Hungary, India, Malaysia, Mexico, the Philippines, Poland, and Russia. Additional low-wage countries studied were Argentina, Bulgaria, Chile, Colombia, Croatia, Estonia, Indonesia, Latvia, Lithuania, Romania, Slovakia, Slovenia, South Africa, Thailand, Turkey, Ukraine, Venezuela, and Vietnam.

5. US Bureau of Labor Statistics.

6. The exception is the pharmaceutical industry, where regulations governing the development of drugs are the main obstacle to offshoring.

7. We included engineers, finance and accounting specialists, generalist professionals, life science researchers, and quantitative analysts, but not doctors, nurses, and general support staff.

8. This figure (13 percent) represents a weighted average, for all low-wage countries, of answers to the interview question, "Of 100 graduates with the correct degree, how many could you employ if you had demand for all?"

9. This is a lower-boundary estimate, since the most suitable job candidates are likely to be the most mobile and to have studied in major cities.

10. Engineers, finance and accounting professionals, quantitative analysts, life science researchers, doctors, nurses, generalists, and support staff.

2

Ensuring India's offshoring future

Diana Farrell, Noshir Kaka, and Sascha Stürze

IDEAS IN BRIEF

India's lead in offshoring stems from its pool of well-trained, low-cost engineers for IT services.

That pool is smaller than it appears, and there's a risk that it may run dry in the most popular offshoring locations.

For offshoring companies, India's weak infrastructure is its most unattractive feature.

India's policy makers must improve the quantity and quality of its graduates, strengthen its infrastructure, and disperse offshore demand for talent to second-tier cities and services other than IT.

ndia's offshoring sector, the world's largest and fastest growing, is dominated by IT services, which play a major role in the country's overall economic growth. In 2004–05, the Indian offshore IT and business-process outsourcing industry will generate approximately $17.3 billion in revenues and employ an estimated 695,000 people. By 2007–08, that workforce will consist of about 1,450,000 to 1,550,000 people, and the industry will account for 7 percent of India's GDP.[1]

Yet clouds are gathering on the offshore horizon. Research by the McKinsey Global Institute (MGI) shows that India's vast supply of graduates is smaller than it seems once their suitability for employment by multinational companies is considered.[2] In the country's most popular offshoring locations, such as Bangalore, rising wages and high turnover among engineers—the professionals most in demand for IT services—provide evidence that local constraints on the supply of talent already exist. And just as these bottlenecks are developing, other low-wage countries, such as China, Hungary, and the Philippines, are gearing up to challenge India's lead.

But the end of India's offshoring bonanza isn't necessarily at hand. India has other attractive qualities beyond low-wage professionals for companies that want to offshore their operations. In 15 years of offshoring, the country has developed a stable of world-class IT services vendors that can save foreign companies the trouble of setting up their own offshore centers. And it has a large supply of qualified talent in areas outside IT, such as R&D, finance and accounting, call centers, and back-office administration.

Still, India's leaders have to ensure that a company hunting for an offshoring location doesn't turn to other countries: the government must not only adjust the country's educational policies to ward off the looming squeeze on talent but also invest more money in infrastructure. So far, offshoring has been largely a private-sector affair, and in some respects the lack of government involvement has been the secret of its success.[3] But private-sector investment in air-conditioned offices, apartments, and shopping malls in offshoring centers has not been matched by public investment in airports, roads, and utilities—improvements necessary to enable the millions of people attracted to these locations to live and work more efficiently. From now on, government and business must work together if offshoring is to remain India's growth engine.

How deep is India's talent pool?

India's pool of young university graduates (those with seven years or less of work experience) is estimated at 14 million—the largest of all 28 countries MGI has studied. It is 1.5 times the size of China's and almost twice that of the United States. This huge number of young graduates is topped up by 2.5 million new ones every year. As in other low-wage countries, however, only a fraction of these people are suited for work in multinational companies.

We interviewed 83 human-resources managers at multinationals that look for talent in the emerging world. Those with experience in India praise the cultural fit and work ethic of their

Indian employees but would still, on average, consider employing only 10 to 25 percent of the country's graduates—a higher proportion of suitable graduates than China produces but only half that of Central Europe. The proportion of suitable graduates also varies by field of study: just 10 percent of the Indian students with generalist degrees in the arts and humanities are suitable, for example, compared with 25 percent of all Indian engineering graduates.[4] Nonetheless, the proportion of suitable engineers in Central Europe is twice as high.

Why is the average level of suitability so low? The answer, largely, is that the quality of India's universities varies a great deal. Graduates of the top schools, such as the seven Indian Institutes of Technology (IITs) and the six Indian Institutes of Management (IIMs), are world-class, but elsewhere the level of quality declines steeply.

One problem is poor English. Although it is an official language in India, not every graduate speaks it well enough to work for the multinationals or for the Indian vendors that serve them. Graduates from certain regions appear to be handicapped by strong local accents that don't lend themselves to jobs in call centers and other workplaces requiring interaction with foreigners. Some companies have relocated call centers from India to the Philippines (where people tend to speak English with an accent closer to that of the US population) because customers complained that they couldn't understand the operators. Even HR managers in software and IT services firms rank language problems as one of the top three handicaps of engineering applicants.

High rates of emigration among graduates of the top schools further depress local supplies of suitable talent. An estimated 40,000 IIT graduates, for example, have gone to work in the United States, though India's buoyant IT services sector is now said to be attracting many of them back.[5] Another hitch is the fact that the country's domestic economy is still largely shielded from global competition, so few older graduates or middle managers have the international experience to switch to the multinationals.

A looming shortage of talent

In India only 1.2 million people hold engineering degrees— 4 percent of the total university-educated workforce, as compared with 20 percent in Germany and 33 percent in China. Combined with the generally low level of suitability among Indian graduates, this means that India could face an overall shortage of engineers in the next few years, with a particular squeeze in certain cities. Wages for India's graduate software engineers have already risen steeply in the most popular offshoring destinations, such as Bangalore and Mumbai.

The country does have a growing number of people who hold engineering diplomas (degrees from three-year rather than four-year programs): 1.75 million in 2003–04, increasing by 130,000 people a year. Diploma holders are not as highly trained as graduates but can fill gaps at the less creative end of the IT value chain. Yet even they will not be sufficiently numerous to alleviate the coming shortages. Our forecasts show that demand for India's young professional engineers is likely to exceed supply by 2008 if current rates of growth in demand (especially from the United Kingdom and the United States) persist. Significant shortfalls of talent are also expected in the field of business-process offshoring, driven by the likelihood that demand and job growth will increase much faster in this industry than they will in IT services over the next three to five years.

The talent squeeze is already beginning to affect the top cities in India, and Hyderabad's recent history shows how fast hot spots can become overheated. The city became a hub for software and IT in the 1990s, when large IT-outsourcing services firms, such as Satyam and Tata Consultancy Services, established themselves there. At least 20 major Indian and US software vendors have set up large engineering centers in Hyderabad since 1998. Activity ballooned after 2002: six new centers, with a total of about 5,000 employees, were established in 2004 alone. Local supplies of suitable candidates for most occupations are ample. But universities and colleges in the Hyderabad region graduate 25,000 engineers a year, which will not be enough to satisfy the demand at current growth rates if only 25 percent are suitable for employment in multinationals. As early as 2006, the demand for suitable engineers will surpass the local supply; by 2008, we reckon, demand will hit 138 percent of supply.

Even so, India's graduates are highly mobile compared with those from other emerging markets. Companies may therefore find that they can easily attract suitable engineers to Hyderabad (in the state of Andra Pradesh) from the country's other cities. Andra Pradesh has been expanding its tertiary-education system unusually quickly since 2001, and the fruits of that expansion have only just begun to reach the labor market. Furthermore, both the state government and local companies are working to improve the suitability and quantity of local graduates and diploma holders. Taking all this into account, Hyderabad may have enough suitable engineers to put off the labor squeeze for a few years beyond 2008. All the same, five years ago no one expected Bangalore and Mumbai to experience the talent shortages they face now. Hyderabad's authorities and companies are right to focus on stepping up the local supply of suitable engineers.

In the country as a whole, middle managers are also becoming scarce. Although India has more of them than other offshoring destinations do, the country also has higher demand because the offshoring sector has grown so fast: over the past decade, the number of middle managers it employs has expanded by more than 20 percent a year, and even more briskly in some cities. New entrants often lure qualified managers from existing businesses instead of training their own. Sometimes they poach across borders as well—Russian entrepreneurs, for example, have hired middle managers from India. Rapidly rising remuneration is evidence of their scarcity. Annual wages for project managers in India's export-oriented IT sector, for instance, have increased, on average, by 23 percent annually over the past four years, while the salaries of programmers have risen by 13 percent (see "On the rise").

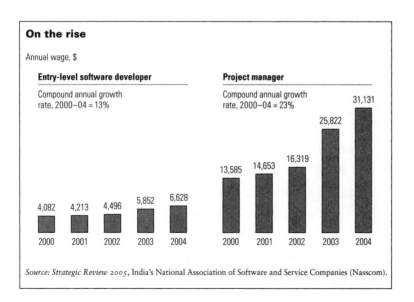

On the rise

Annual wage, $

Entry-level software developer

Compound annual growth rate, 2000–04 = 13%

2000	2001	2002	2003	2004
4,082	4,213	4,496	5,852	6,628

Project manager

Compound annual growth rate, 2000–04 = 23%

2000	2001	2002	2003	2004
13,585	14,653	16,319	25,822	31,131

Source: Strategic Review 2005, India's National Association of Software and Service Companies (Nasscom).

Improving India's offshoring prospects

How can India stay on top of the offshoring ladder? A number of longer-term policy actions must be taken if the country is to remain attractive to companies that want to move their operations offshore—and fixing those aspects of its notoriously weak infrastructure that can hamper a company's efficiency is just one. But in the short term, the priorities for Indian policy makers and for senior managers at companies seeking to offshore operations to India are the squeeze on IT and business-process outsourcing talent in the offshoring hot spots and the looming general shortage of engineering talent.

Raise the quality of university education

To preempt the impending shortage of talent and to increase the supply of graduates suitable for offshoring in general, India must bring more of its fast-growing multitude of graduates up to the level of quality that multinational employers require. Raising the mediocre universities to the standard of the very best will be a tough and lengthy job. Private providers, such as the university-affiliated software-engineering schools of Oracle and Satyam, have driven an explosion in the number of graduates in IT-related disciplines; both private providers and government-funded institutions have contributed to the increasing number of potential candidates for business process jobs.

The central government's policy makers can play an important part in raising standards, by defining curriculums that reflect current and future demand in employment. India's state authorities can help by developing better certification procedures and promoting higher standards of quality for colleges.

Both tiers of government could support the expansion of top-quality private schools.

Companies too can play a role. Private initiatives and joint efforts by companies and universities have helped raise the quality of talent elsewhere in the developing world. In Russia, for instance, associations of software businesses have provided practical management education for engineering students. A recent report from India's National Association of Software and Service Companies (Nasscom) proposed an agenda for improving the suitability of the country's graduates. The agenda included strengthening the collaboration between industry and educational institutions in defining curriculums as well as establishing an IIT in every Indian state.

The vast majority of India's estimated 14 million young university graduates hold generalist degrees, the least attractive ones for multinational employers. Offering grants to study the disciplines—especially engineering—that these companies most covet could also help to raise the proportion of suitable graduates.

Move beyond offshoring hot spots

Wage inflation and high attrition rates in key offshoring locations are understandably making companies nervous about India's supply of talent. But these problems are confined to specific occupations and cities. To some extent, moreover, offshoring companies have created difficulties for themselves by crowding into the same places. Although clustering creates advantages at first, they soon dissipate if demand for talent overwhelms the supply and if infrastructure investments don't keep pace.

Policy makers should encourage companies to look for talent in cities that haven't been touched by the offshoring bandwagon, where cheap supply may well exceed demand. India has huge numbers of skilled graduates in disciplines other than engineering. What's more, MGI research shows that it has the lowest labor cost for university-educated employees of the 16 potential offshore countries we studied (roughly 12 percent of the US cost, on an hourly basis). India's graduates also work the longest hours—on average, 2,350 a year, as compared with 1,900 in the United States and 1,700 in Germany.

Although India's graduates are more mobile than those elsewhere, our estimates show that one-fifth of them still aren't easily accessible to multinationals or Indian service vendors. Indeed, roughly half of the country's graduates study in cities with no international airport. Inaccessibility is a genuine threat to India's offshoring supremacy; our study of supply conditions in 28 low-wage countries shows that many smaller ones have much larger pools of suitable graduates than the size of their populations would suggest (see "Size can be deceptive").[6] India's policy makers must make a priority of helping companies to avail themselves of the country's untapped pockets of supply before too many more of them discover the charms of other offshoring locations. The government may, for instance, have to build airports in less well-known cities and help them with their marketing. Companies exploring these second-tier cities could consider telecommuting as a way of gaining access to additional employees or offer housing deals to get more graduates to move.

Concern about rising wages is somewhat misplaced, however: as a result of local wage inflation, some offshoring companies worry that Indian rates will soon reach US levels. Our projections show that average wages for young professionals in service jobs in India probably won't exceed 30 percent of US levels because of competitive pressures: when average Indian wages reach that threshold, companies will try to employ graduates

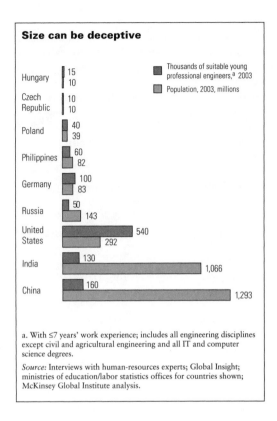

Size can be deceptive

Country	Thousands of suitable young professional engineers,[a] 2003	Population, 2003, millions
Hungary	15	10
Czech Republic	10	10
Poland	40	39
Philippines	60	82
Germany	100	83
Russia	50	143
United States	540	292
India	130	1,066
China	160	1,293

a. With ≤7 years' work experience; includes all engineering disciplines except civil and agricultural engineering and all IT and computer science degrees.

Source: Interviews with human-resources experts; Global Insight; ministries of education/labor statistics offices for countries shown; McKinsey Global Institute analysis.

from countries with lower or comparable wages. Supply from these countries will satisfy all likely demand for the foreseeable future. We therefore do not think that average wages for graduates employed in any of the low-wage countries involved in offshoring, India included, will rise any higher than 30 percent of current wages for young professionals in the United States—about what young professionals in Mexico earn today.

Improve the infrastructure

Our interviews with the multinationals' senior managers show that they rank India's infrastructure as the country's most serious flaw. On a scale of 1 to 5 (good to bad), China rates 2.5 for its infrastructure; India and Russia, each at 3.3, jointly hold last place among the 16 countries we assessed. More direct flights now link Europe with India's offshoring centers, but their poor roads and rudimentary traffic management make local commuting arduous. In 2004 India spent $2 billion on its road network; China spent $30 billion.[7] And despite improvements, India's telecom network still suffers from quality issues.

To stay at the cutting edge of offshoring, India must invest a lot more in its infrastructure—and a lot faster. Government neglect of offshoring may arguably have been benign up to now, but continued neglect of the infrastructure would be a mistake. Only the state can mobilize funds for the airports, communications networks, and utilities that the whole economy requires for healthy future growth.

Move beyond IT and software

India's leaders should start trumpeting its advantages as an offshore location not only for IT but also for industrial R&D and medical research and for back-office functions. This year, the country recognized full product patents on pharmaceuticals. That should reassure international pharma companies, which had feared that any intellectual property they developed in India might not be protected sufficiently. In these new fields, where India offers the requisite talent but is far from having the dominance it enjoys in IT ("Expanding beyond IT"), it would do well to target global companies in the United Kingdom and the United States, which have so far been the pioneers in offshoring.

But in research, India faces stiff competition from China, Russia, and the United States, as R&D often gravitates to countries with large domestic markets for the resulting products.

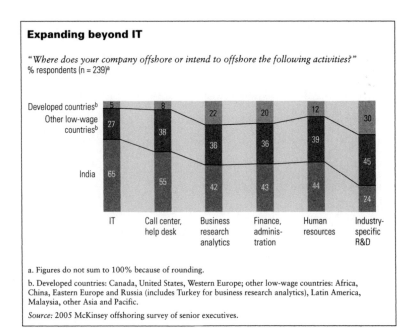

Expanding beyond IT

"Where does your company offshore or intend to offshore the following activities?"
% respondents (n = 239)[a]

	IT	Call center, help desk	Business research analytics	Finance, adminis- tration	Human resources	Industry- specific R&D
Developed countries[b]	5	8	22	20	12	30
Other low-wage countries[b]	27	38	36	36	39	45
India	65	55	42	43	44	24

a. Figures do not sum to 100% because of rounding.

b. Developed countries: Canada, United States, Western Europe; other low-wage countries: Africa, China, Eastern Europe and Russia (includes Turkey for business research analytics), Latin America, Malaysia, other Asia and Pacific.

Source: 2005 McKinsey offshoring survey of senior executives.

India enjoyed annual GDP growth of 6 percent from 2001 to 2004, for a total GDP of around $600 billion, but that isn't enough to offset China's advantage. India also suffers by comparison because of its income distribution. China's wealthy elite is small compared with its large, fast-growing middle class; India's elite is relatively larger, but in 2002 some 74 percent of the country's households earned less than $2,000,[8] which weakens the domestic market's overall purchasing power.

For back-office activities such as finance, HR, analytic and modeling services, and call centers, our projections indicate that India will have enough suitable labor to meet projected demand over the next five years. But the supply of suitable call-center employees will become tighter in some popular locations unless the hiring companies are encouraged to consider other cities. If companies go on crowding into the same few locations made popular by IT services, local wage inflation and high attrition rates will develop even in these new occupations. Policy makers really must try to disperse demand.

Thanks to the dynamism of India's IT services, the country is the world's preeminent offshoring destination. But other low-wage nations are now broadcasting their potential as offshore locations, and demand will quickly exceed India's supply of talent suitable for international companies. To stay on top, India must not only produce more top-quality engineers but also improve the suitability of other graduates. Finally, it has to show companies the depth and quality of its talent in areas other than IT—especially R&D and back-office work in industries such as finance and accounting.

Diana Farrell, Noshir Kaka, and Sascha Stürze,
The McKinsey Quarterly, 2005 Special Edition:
Fulfilling India's promise.

Notes

1. *Strategic Review 2005,* National Association of Software and Service Companies (Nasscom).

2. See the full report, *The Emerging Global Labor Market,* available free of charge at www.mckinsey.com/mgi; or Diana Farrell, Martha A. Laboissère, and Jaeson Rosenfeld, "Sizing the emerging global labor market," *The McKinsey Quarterly,* 2005 Number 3, pp. 92–103 (www.mckinseyquarterly.com/links/18754).

3. Diana Farrell and Adil S. Zainulbhai, "A richer future for India," *The McKinsey Quarterly,* 2004 special edition: *What global executives think,* pp. 26–35 (www.mckinseyquarterly.com/links/18755).

4. Graduates in all engineering disciplines except civil and agricultural engineering.

5. Oliver Ryan, "India's top export: Headed back home?" *Fortune,* June 13, 2005.

6. Diana Farrell, Martha A. Laboissière, and Jaeson Rosenfeld, "Sizing the emerging global labor market," *The McKinsey Quarterly,* 2005 Number 3, pp. 92–103 (www.mckinseyquarterly.com/links/18754).

7. Edward Luce, "India to dip into forex reserves to build roads," *Financial Times,* October 16, 2004.

8. "The insidious charm of foreign investment," *Economist,* March 3, 2005.

3

China's looming talent shortage

Diana Farrell and Andrew J. Grant

IDEAS IN BRIEF

If China's economy is to go on growing and its base is to evolve from manufacturing to services, it will require a huge number of qualified university graduates.

While university graduates are plentiful there, new MGI research shows that only a small proportion of them have the skills required for jobs further up the value chain—and competition for these graduates is becoming fierce.

China must undertake a long-term effort to raise the quality of its graduates by changing the way it finances its universities, revamping curricula to meet the needs of industry and improving the quality of English-language instruction.

China could emerge as a base for IT and business-process offshoring, but unless the country addresses its looming labor shortage now, the global ambitions of Chinese companies will probably be stymied.

With a huge supply of low-cost workers, mainland China has fast become the world's manufacturing workshop, supplying everything from textiles to toys to computer chips. Given the country's millions of university graduates, is it set to become a giant in offshore IT and business-process services as well.

New research from the McKinsey Global Institute (MGI) suggests that this outcome is unlikely.[1] The reason: few of China's vast number of university graduates are capable of working successfully in the services export sector, and the fast-growing domestic economy absorbs most of those who could. Indeed, far from presaging a thriving offshore services sector, our research points to a looming shortage of homegrown talent, with serious implications for the multinationals now in China and for the growing number of Chinese companies with global ambitions.

If China is to avoid this talent crunch and to sustain its economic ascent, it must produce more graduates fit for employment in world-class companies, whether local or foreign. Raising the graduates' quality will allow the economy to evolve from its present domination by manufacturing and toward a future in which services play the leading role—as they eventually must when any economy develops and matures. The conditions for a flourishing offshore services sector will then surely follow.

The supply paradox

China's pool of potential talent is enormous. In 2003 China had roughly 9.6 million young professional graduates with up to seven years' work experience and an additional 97 million people who would qualify for support-staff positions.

Despite this apparently vast supply, multinational companies are finding that few graduates have the necessary skills for service occupations. According to interviews with 83 human-resources professionals involved with hiring local graduates in low-wage countries, fewer than 10 percent of Chinese job candidates, on average, would be suitable for work in a foreign company in the nine occupations we studied: engineers, finance workers, accountants, quantitative analysts, generalists, life science researchers, doctors, nurses, and support staff.

Consider engineers. China has 1.6 million young ones, more than any other country we examined.[2] Indeed, 33 percent of the university students in China study engineering,[3] compared with 20 percent in Germany and just 4 percent in India. But the main drawback of Chinese applicants for engineering jobs, our interviewees said, is the educational system's bias toward theory. Compared with engineering graduates in Europe and North America, who work in teams to achieve practical solutions, Chinese students get little practical experience in projects or teamwork. The result of these differences is that China's pool of young engineers considered suitable for work in multinationals is just 160,000—no larger than the United Kingdom's. Hence the paradox of shortages amid plenty.

For jobs in the eight other occupations we studied, poor English was the main reason our interviewees gave for rejecting Chinese applicants. Only 3 percent of them can be considered for generalist service positions (those that don't require a degree in any particular subject). Overall communication style and cultural fit are also difficult hurdles. One Chinese HR professional points out, for example, that Chinese software engineers would find it hard to draw up an information flowchart for an international five-star hotel, not because they don't understand flowcharts, but because state-run hotels in China—the only ones they know—are so very different.[4] Some people argue that a willingness to work long hours will compensate for any deficiencies in the suitability of China's talent. Although this may hold true to some extent in manufacturing, it is likely to make only a marginal difference in services because of the specific skill deficiencies that come into play.

On top of the generally low suitability of Chinese graduates, they are widely dispersed. Well over 1,500 colleges and universities produced the 1.7 million students who graduated in 2003, and likely less than one-third of them had studied in any of the top ten university cities (see "Scattered scholars"). Just one-quarter

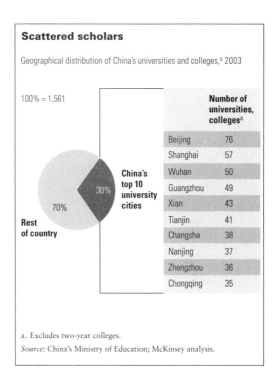

Scattered scholars

Geographical distribution of China's universities and colleges,[a] 2003

100% = 1,561

	Number of universities, colleges[a]
Beijing	76
Shanghai	57
Wuhan	50
Guangzhou	49
Xian	43
Tianjin	41
Changsha	38
Nanjing	37
Zhengzhou	36
Chongqing	35

China's top 10 university cities — 30%

Rest of country — 70%

a. Excludes two-year colleges.

Source: China's Ministry of Education; McKinsey analysis.

of all Chinese graduates live in a city or region close to a major international airport—a requirement of most multinationals setting up offshore facilities. Compounding that problem is a lack of mobility: only one-third of all Chinese graduates move to other provinces for work. (By contrast, almost half of all Indian students graduate close to a major international hub, such as Bangalore, Delhi, Hyderabad, and Mumbai, and most are quite willing to move.) As a result of these two factors, world-class companies that want to hire service labor in China have difficulty reaching as much as half of the total pool of graduates.

Finally, companies that wish to set up services offshoring operations in China face more competition for talent than they would in other low-wage locations. In India and the Philippines, for example, the local economy is growing less briskly, and working for a company that provides offshore services is therefore a good option. In China, domestic and multinational companies serving the fast-growing domestic market already provide attractive opportunities for suitable graduates, and there are many more jobs in the manufacturing export sector. As a result, it's wrong to assume, as many companies do, that every suitable young professional in China is available for hire in the services offshoring sector.

The looming war for talent

More crucially, companies that are already in China and serve its fast-growing domestic market will also, our research shows, have difficulty finding enough suitable employees in key service and managerial occupations.

The demand for labor from just the large foreign-owned companies and joint ventures that now do business in China highlights the problem.[5] From 1998 to 2002, employment in these two categories rose by 12 and 23 percent a year, respectively, to about 2.7 million workers. Assuming that 30 percent of these workers must have at least a college degree[6] and that the labor demands of such companies continue to grow at the same rates, they will have to employ an additional 750,000 graduates from 2003 through 2008. China, we estimate, will produce 1.2 million graduates suitable for employment in world-class service companies during that period. So large foreign multinationals and joint ventures alone will take up to 60 percent of China's suitable graduates before demand from smaller multinationals or Chinese companies even enters the picture (see "A shortage of suitable candidates").

If these numbers suggest fierce competition for China's best graduates, unemployment statistics confirm that impression. In 2003 just 1 percent of the country's university graduates were unemployed—an almost negligible rate. Unemployment among the graduates of China's colleges is a bit higher, at about 6 percent.

Effective managers are in short supply as well. We estimate that given the global aspirations of many Chinese companies, over the next 10 to 15 years they will need 75,000 leaders who can work effectively in global environments; today they have only 3,000 to 5,000.[7] Management talent generally comes from several sources—offshoring enterprises that train lower-level workers, industries that produce managers with relevant skills, and expatriates who have worked or studied in countries with developed economies. But people from all of these sources are scarce in China. Although multinational companies there do currently train and promote managers from entry-level positions, the process is time-consuming and costly. Moreover, with levels of foreign direct investment so high, multinationals often

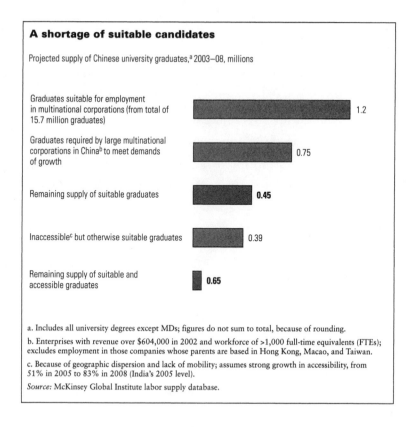

A shortage of suitable candidates

Projected supply of Chinese university graduates,[a] 2003–08, millions

Graduates suitable for employment in multinational corporations (from total of 15.7 million graduates)	1.2
Graduates required by large multinational corporations in China[b] to meet demands of growth	0.75
Remaining supply of suitable graduates	**0.45**
Inaccessible[c] but otherwise suitable graduates	0.39
Remaining supply of suitable and accessible graduates	**0.65**

a. Includes all university degrees except MDs; figures do not sum to total, because of rounding.

b. Enterprises with revenue over $604,000 in 2002 and workforce of >1,000 full-time equivalents (FTEs); excludes employment in those companies whose parents are based in Hong Kong, Macao, and Taiwan.

c. Because of geographic dispersion and lack of mobility; assumes strong growth in accessibility, from 51% in 2005 to 83% in 2008 (India's 2005 level).

Source: McKinsey Global Institute labor supply database.

resort to poaching from each other. The problem is all the worse because not many middle managers can be hired from Chinese companies; only people employed by very high-performing ones (such as the consumer electronics company TCL) have the skills and cultural attributes needed to work for the multinationals. A more plentiful source of middle-management talent is the large number of ethnic Chinese who fill management roles for companies in Hong Kong, Singapore, and Taiwan. These people can be recruited to mainland China but often require "local-plus" packages: wages and benefits above what the locals receive, though less than the full expatriate package.

Why fix the problem?

A shortage of world-class university graduates in key occupations such as finance, accounting, engineering, and business represents a major problem for multinationals in China, for Chinese companies, and for the country's policy makers. Companies need these graduates to improve their marketing and product-development efforts, to understand consumer tastes, to develop customer service and after-sales-service operations, and to raise their local financial and accounting standards. In the longer term, China's economy as a whole needs more such graduates if it is to compete in the world beyond the simpler, labor-intensive manufacturing areas in which it is now the global leader.

As economies develop, they shift from labor-intensive manufacturing to higher-value areas, notably marketing, product design, and the manufacture of sophisticated intermediate inputs. Northern Italy's textile and apparel industry, for example, has moved most garment production to lower-cost locations, but employment remains stable because companies have put more resources into tasks such as designing clothes and coordinating global production networks. Similarly, in the US automotive industry, imports of finished cars from Mexico increased rapidly after the North American Free Trade Agreement took effect, but at the same time exports of US auto parts to Mexico have quadrupled, allowing much of the more capital-intensive work—and many of the higher-paid jobs—to remain in the United States.[8]

With an estimated 150 million surplus unskilled rural workers,[9] who can be hired mainly by manufacturers, China is decades away from developing a consumer-oriented service economy. But policy makers must make that their ultimate aspiration. No nation will remain the world's low-cost manufacturer forever, and if it were to try to do so, its living standards would stagnate at today's levels—or even decline. Today China's economy is greatly tilted toward manufacturing, and the services sector is notably underdeveloped (see "China's underdeveloped services sector"). But in China, as in all economies, services will be the future engine of job growth. According to Alliance Capital

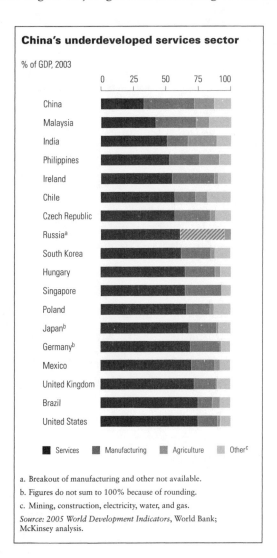

China's underdeveloped services sector

% of GDP, 2003

Legend: ■ Services ■ Manufacturing ■ Agriculture ■ Other[c]

(Countries listed top to bottom: China, Malaysia, India, Philippines, Ireland, Chile, Czech Republic, Russia[a], South Korea, Hungary, Singapore, Poland, Japan[b], Germany[b], Mexico, United Kingdom, Brazil, United States)

a. Breakout of manufacturing and other not available.
b. Figures do not sum to 100% because of rounding.
c. Mining, construction, electricity, water, and gas.

Source: 2005 World Development Indicators, World Bank; McKinsey analysis.

Management, the country's manufacturing sector shed 15 million jobs from 1995 to 2002, when large state-owned factories restructured their operations. As manufacturing productivity rises, still more jobs will be lost.

Creating the conditions that attract offshore services operations will help China move up the ladder. The country does have some strong advantages in this arena, notably low labor costs, an enormous domestic market, and a relatively high-quality infrastructure. Offshore services activities are often developed from existing operations, so China's services offshoring sector is most likely to arise as an offshoot of the activities of companies that are already there.

Pharmaceutical and software companies will probably take the lead, for in these industries some multinationals have already set up Chinese R&D operations to customize products for local needs. Several players now use incremental capacity in their Chinese R&D facilities to serve overseas markets too. Pharma companies can also run bigger, and therefore faster, clinical trials in China more cheaply, thereby cutting overall product-development costs as well as approval and release times. In addition, mainland China could emerge as a base for business-process offshoring by multinationals that serve Chinese-speaking populations elsewhere—such as Hong Kong, Singapore, and Taiwan—if the country solves its looming shortage of qualified labor.

Addressing the shortage

Raising the quality of China's graduates will be a long-term effort, but even modest improvements would make a huge difference. If the proportion of Chinese engineering graduates who could work at global companies increased to 25 percent (as it is in India) from today's 10 percent, China's pool of qualified young engineers would be among the world's largest by 2008.

How can the country raise the quality of its graduates? First, it must change the way it finances its universities. Expenditures for tertiary education are growing quite rapidly—from 2000 to 2002, by more than 50 percent. The number of students increased even more, however, so expenditures per student fell by 5 percent. Funding is also spread unevenly throughout the country: in Beijing average spending per student is more than 30 percent higher than it is in second-place Shanghai and more than twice the level in 25 of the 31 provinces. More money should be focused on raising quality than quantity, and funds for institutions in places other than Beijing and Shanghai should rise dramatically.

In addition, China must continue to improve its English-language instruction. Since 2001, the Ministry of Education has required all students to start learning English in third grade. This is a step in the right direction and will pay dividends in the long run, but English classes are still very large, even at universities, because teachers are in short supply.[10] Furthermore, conversational skills receive too little attention. To resolve both of these issues, China must train many more English teachers and do more to recruit them from abroad.

For the foreseeable future, companies themselves will have to invest more in training and developing the talent they need. When Microsoft, for instance, outsourced part of its Web-based technical support to Shanghai Wicresoft, a 400-employee joint venture with the Shanghai municipal government, it hired ten native US English speakers to teach their Chinese coworkers about US e-mail protocol and writing style. These instructors hold language classes and meet one-on-one with Chinese employees to assess their progress, an effort that raises the joint venture's personnel costs by about 15 percent[11] but brings the language skills of Chinese workers up to speed. Other foreign companies are developing management-training courses, sometimes in collaboration with local business schools, to upgrade the skills of existing middle and top managers.[12]

Companies can also work with policy makers and university leaders to bring curricula—not only at the top universities but also throughout the university system—more in line with the needs of industry. Software projects are team efforts that require less theoretical knowledge than application skills, which Chinese graduates lack, according to managers at multinational companies. In response, Microsoft has formed partnerships with four universities in China to establish software labs where student interns learn practical software-development skills. Other companies should adopt similar policies. Such public-private education programs make students more suitable for good jobs with world-class companies and ease the transition to middle-management roles later on.

Finally, China's policy makers must ensure that its many students who study abroad return home, since a relatively high proportion of them have the skills needed to work for multinationals. In 2003, some 120,000 Chinese students were studying abroad—the highest number of any of the 28 countries whose supply of graduates MGI has investigated. Moreover, half of these Chinese students were living in the United States, the largest overseas market linked to China. India's diaspora, including people who have returned to their homeland, has played an important role in the growth of the Indian IT and business-process services sector while helping to alleviate the country's management shortage. China too needs its expats.

China faces a looming labor shortage that could stall not only its economic growth but also its migration up the value chain. Reforms in the educational system—including a greater emphasis on practical and language skills—will help the country fill its skilled-labor gap.

The authors would like to acknowledge the contributions of Martha Laboissière, Jaeson Rosenfeld, Sascha Stürze, and Fusayo Umezawa.

Diana Farrell and Andrew J. Grant,
The McKinsey Quarterly, 2005 Number 4.

Notes

1. The full report, *The Emerging Global Labor Market,* is available free of charge at www.mckinsey.com/mgi.

2. The low-wage countries we studied were Argentina, Brazil, Bulgaria, Chile, China, Colombia, Croatia, the Czech Republic, Estonia, Hungary, India, Indonesia, Latvia, Lithuania, Malaysia, Mexico, the Philippines, Poland, Romania, Russia, Slovakia, Slovenia, South Africa, Thailand, Turkey, Ukraine, Venezuela, and Vietnam. The mid- to high-wage countries we studied in depth were Canada, Germany, Ireland, Japan, the United Kingdom, and the United States; Australia and South Korea were studied by way of extrapolation.

3. All branches except civil and agricultural engineering.

4. Juhi Bhambal, interview with Alan Choi, Korn/Ferry's regional managing director for Greater China, *Global Outsourcing,* January 11, 2005 (www.globaloutsourcing.org).

5. We considered only companies with more than 1,000 employees. Foreign-owned companies in Hong Kong, Macao, and Taiwan were excluded.

6. This estimate is based on MGI's study of the global automotive industry, where 48 percent of all jobs require a college education. Since the estimate includes headquarters functions, we reduced it to 30 percent.

7. Andrew Grant and Georges Desvaux, "Narrowing China's corporate-leadership gap," *China Daily,* May 18, 2005.

8. Diana Farrell, Antonio Puron, and Jaana K. Remes, "Beyond cheap labor: Lessons for developing economies," *The McKinsey Quarterly,* 2005 Number 1, pp. 98–109 (www.mckinseyquarterly.com/links/19110).

9. "Surplus rural laborers hit 150 million," Xinhua News Agency, April 8, 2004 (www.china.org.cn).

10. Yuan-yuan Huang and Hua-li Xu, "Trends in English language education in China," *ESL Magazine,* November/December 1999.

11. Li Yuan, "Chinese companies vie for a role in US IT outsourcing," *Wall Street Journal,* April 5, 2005.

12. McKinsey will pilot such a program in early 2006.

4

Who wins in offshoring?

Vivek Agrawal and Diana Farrell

IDEAS IN BRIEF

Companies in the United States that optimize their earnings through offshoring are creating a net increase in wealth for *both* countries involved.

Offshoring returns significant direct benefits to the US economy in the form of cost savings, new revenues, and repatriated earnings, and indirectly helps to create new jobs for displaced workers.

Flexibility in US labor markets and the mobility of US workers make it possible for the United States to create new jobs faster than offshoring eliminates them, over the medium term.

However, companies and the government should invest in mitigating the difficulties of those employees displaced by offshoring who can find only lower-paid replacement work, or no new job at all.

Widely cited figures predict that by 2015, roughly 3.3 million US business-processing jobs will have moved abroad.[1] As of July 2003, around 400,000 jobs already had. Other research suggests that the number of US service jobs lost to offshoring will accelerate at a rate of 30 to 40 percent annually during the next five years.[2] Vast wage differentials are prompting companies to move their labor-intensive service jobs to countries with low labor costs: for instance, software developers, who cost $60 an hour in the United States, the world's biggest offshorer, cost only $6 an hour in India, the biggest market for offshored services.

Such projections have caused alarm in the United States. In February 2003, the cover of *BusinessWeek* asked, "Is your job next?" In June, the US House of Representatives' Committee on Small Business held a hearing on "The globalization of white-collar jobs: Can America lose these jobs and still prosper?" Several US states are considering legislation to prohibit or severely restrict their state governments from contracting with companies that move jobs to low-wage developing countries,[3] and labor unions, notably the Communications Workers of America, are lobbying Congress to prevent offshoring. Yet pandering to protectionism would be wrong. Many people believe that money spent to buy services abroad is lost to the US economy, but such views are easily disproved. Companies move their business services offshore because they can make more money—which means that wealth is created for the United States as well as for the country receiving the jobs. A McKinsey Global Institute (MGI) study reveals the extent of the mutual benefits.[4]

As the study shows, for every dollar that was previously spent on business processes in the United States and now goes to India, India earns a net benefit of at least 33 cents, in the form of government taxes,[5] wages paid by US companies, and revenues earned by Indian vendors of business-process services and their suppliers (see "Offshoring's value to India"). What of the impact on the US economy? First, it is important to put the figures in context, since fear of job losses makes many people overstate the effects of offshoring. Some 70 percent of jobs in the United States are in service industries such as retailing, catering, and personal care. This work, by its very nature, cannot be moved abroad.

In addition, any job losses must be seen as part of an ongoing process of economic restructuring, with which the US economy is well acquainted. Technological change, economic recessions,

Offshoring's value to India

Benefit per $1 of US offshore spending,[a] 2002, $

Offshoring sector	Labor	0.10
	Profits retained in India	0.10
Suppliers[b]		0.09
Taxes	Central government[c]	0.03
	State government[d]	0.01
	Net benefit to India	**0.33**

a. Estimated; India offshore services industry example.

b. Includes revenue accruing to supplier industries less sales taxes, income taxes for employees, and corporate taxes.

c. Includes income tax from labor employed in both offshore services sector and supplier industries as well as corporate tax on second- and third-tier suppliers.

d. Includes sales tax on second- and third-tier suppliers and revenue from sale of power to offshore service providers (providers' earnings are tax-exempt).

shifts in consumer demand, business restructuring, and public policy (including trade liberalization and environmental regulation) can and frequently do result in job losses. Even when the economy is growing, mass layoffs—usually from restructuring— are much higher than the job losses predicted from offshoring.[6] In 1999, for instance, 1.15 million workers lost jobs through mass layoffs, out of a total of 2.5 million lost. Liberalized, competitive economies with flexible labor markets can usually cope with such restructuring; the US economy, the world's most dynamic, certainly should be able to do so. Indeed, history suggests that, over the medium to long term, a flexible job market and the mobility of US workers will make it possible for the United States to create new jobs faster than offshoring eliminates them.

The United States today has more than 130 million employed workers. According to the Organisation for Economic Co-operation and Development, it has the highest rate of reemployment of any OECD country by a factor of almost two. Over the past ten years, 3.5 million private-sector jobs a year have been created, on average, for a total of 35 million new jobs, so most workers who lose their positions find another within six months. Jobs lost to low-cost foreign competitors are not so easy to replace. Nonetheless, from 1979 to 1999, 69 percent of the people who lost jobs as a result of cheap imports in sectors other than manufacturing were reemployed.[7] The mean wage of those reemployed was 96.2 percent of their previous wage.

Finally, remember that the population of the United States is aging. At current productivity levels, the country will need 5 percent, or 15.6 million, more workers by 2015 to maintain both its current ratio of workers to the total population and its living standards. By 2015, despite current fears about job losses as a result of offshoring, the US economy will need more, not fewer, workers. Offshoring is one way to meet that need.

But focusing the offshoring debate on job losses misses the most important point: offshoring creates value for the US economy by creating value for US companies and freeing US resources for activities with more value added. It creates value in four ways:

- *Cost savings.* For every dollar of spending on business services that moves offshore, US companies save 58 cents, mainly in wages. Offshore services are identical to those they replace—and at times better, since offshore workers, enjoying higher-than-usual wages, tend to be motivated. Reduced costs are by far the greatest source of value creation for the US economy.

- *New revenues.* Indian companies that provide offshore services need goods and services themselves, ranging from computers and telecommunications equipment to legal, financial, and marketing expertise. Often, they buy these from US companies. We estimate that for every dollar of corporate spending that moves offshore, suppliers of offshore services buy an additional five cents' worth of goods and services in the United States. Exports from the United States to India stood at $4.1 billion in 2002, compared with less than $2.5 billion in 1990.

- *Repatriated earnings.* Many Indian offshore service providers are in fact US companies that repatriate earnings. Such companies generate 30 percent of the revenues of the Indian offshore industry. Thus an additional four cents of every dollar spent on offshoring creates value for the United States.

- *Redeployed labor.* Beyond the direct benefits to the United States in the form of savings, new exports, and repatriated profits, offshoring can indirectly benefit the economy: capital savings can be invested to create new jobs for which labor will be available. Indeed, this is exactly what has happened over the past two decades as manufacturing jobs moved offshore. The Bureau of Labor Statistics reports that overall manufacturing employment shrank by two million jobs in the past 20 years. But workers have found it easy to locate jobs in other areas, such as educational and health services. These service jobs, on average, pay more than the manufacturing ones they replaced, helping to increase the population's standard of living.

The same thing could well happen again. As jobs in call centers, back-office operations, and repetitive IT functions go offshore, opportunities to train labor and invest capital to generate opportunities in higher-value-added occupations such as research and design will appear. The Bureau of Labor Statistics estimates that from 2000 to 2010, there will be a net creation of about 22 million new jobs in the economy, mostly in business services, health care, social services, transportation, and communications. (See "Offshoring's value to the United States").

How much value will be created in this way depends on the country's future economic performance. Historical trends can serve as a guide. If we use the statistics on reemployment and wage levels already noted—69 percent of nonmanufacturing workers are reemployed at 96.2 percent of their previous wages—and bear in mind that 72 cents of every dollar offshored had previ-

Offshoring's value to the United States

Benefit per $1 of US spending sent offshore,[a] 2002, $

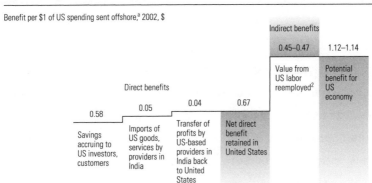

a. Estimated; India offshore services industry example.

b. Conservative estimate based on historical reemployment and wage levels; value created from improved global competitiveness of US companies and multiplier effect of increased savings would likely increase amount of value created.

ously been spent on US wages,[8] the indirect benefit to the US economy would come to an additional 45 to 47 cents for every dollar spent on offshoring. That is a conservative estimate, since workers in IT and business services tend to find jobs more quickly than do workers in the service sector as a whole, and the demographic shift will increase the demand for workers.

In this way, offshoring, far from being bad for the United States, creates net value for the economy. It directly recaptures 67 cents of every dollar of spending that goes abroad and indirectly might capture an additional 45 to 47 cents—producing a net gain of 12 to 14 cents for every dollar of costs moved offshore.

The total possible wealth creation does not, of course, ease the plight of people who lose their jobs or find lower-wage ones. The statistics showing that 69 percent of those who lost jobs in the nonmanufacturing sector were reemployed also show that

31 percent were *not* fully reemployed. And while, on average, those who found new jobs secured similar wages (96.2 percent of their previous wage), 55 percent took lower-paid jobs. As many as 25 percent took pay cuts of 30 percent or more.

These issues must be addressed. Training programs and generous severance packages, perhaps accompanied by innovative insurance programs (see "Easing the pain for workers"), are among the measures that could mitigate the effects of the transition without great cost to the economy. And while many people will undoubtedly suffer short-term disruption, it should be set against the consequences of resisting change: if US companies can't move work abroad they will become less competitive—weakening the economy and endangering more jobs—and miss the chance to raise their productivity by focusing on the creation of jobs with higher value added.

The openness of the US economy and its inherent flexibility—particularly that of its labor market—are two of its great recognized strengths. The current danger is that public policy will make its economy less flexible. To do so would endanger the economic well-being of the United States.

Easing the pain for workers

As part of severance packages, and for a small percentage of the savings from offshoring, companies could purchase insurance covering the wage losses of displaced workers. Building upon an insurance proposal that Lori Kletzer (of the University of California, Santa Cruz) and Robert Litan (of the Brookings Institution) developed for workers displaced by trade in manufacturing,[a] the

McKinsey Global Institute estimates that for as little as 4 to 5 percent of the savings companies realized from offshoring, they could insure all full-time workers who lost jobs as a result. The program would compensate those workers for 70 percent of the wages they missed from the time they were laid off to the time they were reemployed, as well as offer health care subsidies for up to two years.

---

a. Lori Kletzer and Robert Litan, "A prescription to relieve worker anxiety," Policy Brief 01-2, Institute for International Economics, February 2001.

Vivek Agrawal and Diana Farrell,
McKinsey Quarterly, 2003 Special Edition: *Global directions.*

Notes

1. An estimate by the IT research firm Forrester.

2. A consensus estimate of the market research firms Aberdeen Group, Gartner, and IDC.

3. "States fight exodus of jobs," *Wall Street Journal*, June 3, 2003.

4. The study estimated the distribution of revenues from the $8 billion in services offshored to India. Estimates were compiled from industry interviews and published reports on both the demand and the supply sides.

5. Taxes are collected from second- and third-tier suppliers to the service providers as well as on wages earned by labor. The providers themselves enjoy tax-free status in India.

6. The Bureau of Labor Statistics defines a mass layoff as 50 or more worker claims against an establishment's unemployment-insurance account during a five-week period.

7. See Lori Kletzer, *Job Loss from Imports: Measuring the Costs,* Washington, DC: Institute for International Economics, 2001. Kletzer matched Bureau of Labor Statistics figures on nonmanufacturing jobs with trade data to assess job displacement in sectors prone to foreign competition.

8. Of every dollar spent, 72 cents goes to wages and the rest to equipment, furnishings, rent, utilities, financing, and other services.

5

The truth about foreign direct investment in emerging markets

Diana Farrell, Jaana K. Remes, and Heiner Schulz

IDEAS IN BRIEF

Our studies of the local effects of foreign direct investment in a range of industries and countries show that the receiving economies realize significant benefits from FDI in the form of higher market output, productivity, and standards of living.

Incentives used by developing countries to entice multinationals and restrictions they use to protect local industry are largely ineffective and often counterproductive.

Money spent to improve local infrastructure and economic stability maximizes foreign investment more effectively than direct incentives.

Regulations requiring foreign firms to use local industry inputs tend to backfire by reducing local firms' competitiveness, making the economy in question less attractive to investors.

A surge in activity by multinationals in the developing world has opened a new chapter in globalization. What was once a marginal activity in emerging markets has now become essential to the competitiveness and growth of many foreign companies. In 2002 they invested $162 billion in the developing world, up from just $15 billion in 1985. Today their investments are worth more than $2 trillion and growing.

Governments in emerging markets are understandably eager to have their share of this foreign capital, along with the technology and management skills that accompany it. Foreign companies get a smorgasbord of tax holidays, import duty exemptions, subsidized land and power, and other enticements, all offered by developing countries in the belief that this is the way to attract multinationals. For every job created, the incentives may add up to tens of thousands of dollars annually—in some cases, more than $200,000 in net present value.

Yet even as developing nations dole out lucrative incentives to attract foreign investment, they are often wary of multinational companies. Attempting to protect domestic industry and to ensure that foreign investment benefits the local economy, many of these nations restrict the way foreign companies can operate.

But new research from the McKinsey Global Institute (MGI) finds that both the incentives used to attract foreign direct investment and the restrictions placed on it are largely ineffective.[1] Worse, they are frequently counterproductive, costing governments millions of dollars annually, protecting inefficient players, and lowering living standards and productivity. Our research shows that regardless of the policy regime, the industry, or the period studied, foreign direct investment can benefit developing nations greatly. To make the most of it, however, they must strengthen the foundations of their economies, including the infrastructure, the legal and regulatory environment, and the level of competition.

It's good for emerging markets

Foreign direct investment by multinational companies in emerging markets is perhaps the most controversial form of globalization. Critics, who charge that foreign companies exploit poor workers and flout labor laws, tend to focus on the reported abuses. Defenders, arguing that foreign investment brings new capital, technology, and jobs to countries that need them, rely on macroeconomic data and econometric approaches that at best yield qualified answers.

To bring new facts to this often emotional debate, we calculated the impact of foreign direct investment on local industries—manufacturing and service alike—in Brazil, China, India, and Mexico. The industries included automotive, banking, consumer electronics, food retailing, and IT and business-process outsourcing. In each of our 14 industry studies, we looked at industry dynamics, sector productivity, output, employment, and prices before and after foreign companies entered the market. We also conducted interviews with foreign and local executives.

In 13 of our 14 cases, foreign direct investment unambiguously helped the receiving economy (see "Unambiguously positive"). It raised productivity and output in the sectors involved, thereby raising national income while lowering prices and improving the quality and selection of services and products for

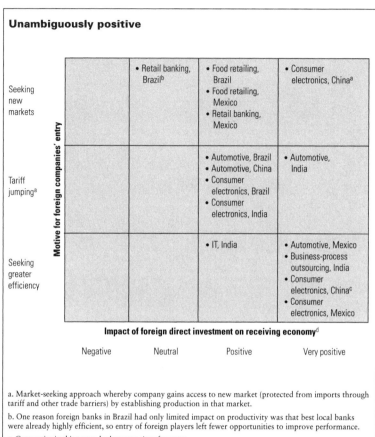

Unambiguously positive

Motive for foreign companies' entry	Negative	Neutral	Positive	Very positive
Seeking new markets		• Retail banking, Brazil[b]	• Food retailing, Brazil • Food retailing, Mexico • Retail banking, Mexico	• Consumer electronics, China[a]
Tariff jumping[a]			• Automotive, Brazil • Automotive, China • Consumer electronics, Brazil • Consumer electronics, India	• Automotive, India
Seeking greater efficiency			• IT, India	• Automotive, Mexico • Business-process outsourcing, India • Consumer electronics, China[c] • Consumer electronics, Mexico

Impact of foreign direct investment on receiving economy[d]

a. Market-seeking approach whereby company gains access to new market (protected from imports through tariff and other trade barriers) by establishing production in that market.

b. One reason foreign banks in Brazil had only limited impact on productivity was that best local banks were already highly efficient, so entry of foreign players left fewer opportunities to improve performance.

c. Companies in this sector had two motives for entry.

d. Qualitative measure based on combination of productivity, sector output, level of employment/wages, and consumer prices/ product selection, among others.

consumers. Rather than being beneficial only in certain cases, foreign investment nearly always generated positive spillovers for the rest of the economy.

The standard of living improves

Perhaps the biggest benefit of foreign direct investment—and one seldom discussed—is its ability to raise local standards of living. We estimate, contrary to popular perceptions, that around

80 percent of foreign investments today are made by companies that enter local markets and sell goods there, not by companies that produce cheap goods for export. Carrefour, for example, is opening stores in Brazil, Citibank is setting up branches in Mexico, and Suzuki Motor is building and selling cars in India.

Local consumers are the biggest beneficiaries of market-seeking investment. In nearly every one of our case studies, they enjoyed lower prices or a better selection of goods and services—or both—after foreign companies arrived. The price of passenger cars in China, for instance, declined by more than 30 percent from 1995 to 2001, years when Ford Motor, GM, and Honda Motor entered the market. (But tariffs still keep prices there much higher than they should be.) In Mexico, Wal-Mart's "everyday low prices" ended a long history of hefty margins for the country's leading retailers to such an extent that some analysts now credit the company with helping to reduce the country's inflation rate. In India, the price of air conditioners, televisions, and washing machines fell by around 10 percent in 2001 alone after foreign companies entered the market.

Prices fall because foreign players improve a sector's efficiency and productivity by bringing in new capital, technology, and management skills and by forcing less efficient domestic companies either to improve their operations or to exit. Although some incumbents stand to lose market share, consumers benefit from lower prices, which in many cases lead to a boom in demand and to the creation of new wealth.

Consider the Indian automotive industry. Until the early 1980s, the protected local market was dominated by two highly inefficient players: Hindustan Motors (HM) and PAL, which offered just two car models, based on 1960s technology and priced at around $20,000. In 1983, the government allowed Suzuki to set up a joint venture with Maruti Udyog, a state-owned enterprise. Within a few years, eight car models were for sale and the quality of all cars on the market, including those from HM and PAL, had improved dramatically. The government lifted many remaining barriers against foreign manufacturers in 1992 and 12 of them entered the market. Since then, the sector's productivity levels have continued to rise rapidly, in part because of PAL's exit ("Competition boosts productivity"). Today at least 30 car models are sold in India, and prices in all segments have steadily declined by 8 to 10 percent a year. As a result, local demand has exploded and the industry has tripled in size.

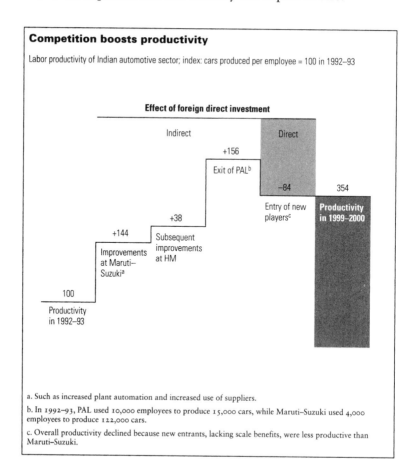

Competition boosts productivity

Labor productivity of Indian automotive sector; index: cars produced per employee = 100 in 1992–93

Effect of foreign direct investment

Indirect

+156

Exit of PAL[b]

Direct

−84

354

Entry of new players[c]

Productivity in 1999–2000

+38

+144

Subsequent improvements at HM

Improvements at Maruti–Suzuki[a]

100

Productivity in 1992–93

a. Such as increased plant automation and increased use of suppliers.

b. In 1992–93, PAL used 10,000 employees to produce 15,000 cars, while Maruti–Suzuki used 4,000 employees to produce 122,000 cars.

c. Overall productivity declined because new entrants, lacking scale benefits, were less productive than Maruti–Suzuki.

Good jobs are created

Globalization's most vocal critics often focus on another type of foreign direct investment, made by companies seeking to produce goods cheaply and to export them. We found, however, that such efficiency-seeking investments are even more unambiguously positive for the local economy because they create jobs and boost output without threatening domestic companies.

Foreign direct investment in India, for instance, has contributed to the creation of a more than $10-billion-a-year software and outsourcing industry, which employs 500,000 people who perform white-collar jobs for foreign companies. Projections suggest that it will employ 2 million people by 2008. In Mexico, the *maquiladoras* along the US border employ 1.1 million workers who assemble consumer electronics and other goods for export to the United States. In China, multinational companies have spurred the growth of a consumer electronics sector that now employs 863,000 people and generates $1.7 billion a year in net export revenues.

Contrary to what critics charge, our case studies showed that in every instance foreign companies, both export oriented and not, paid wages that were at least equivalent to, and in most cases higher than, the wages offered by their domestic competitors. Wages in India's business-process outsourcing sector, for instance, are 50 to 100 percent higher than those in other white-collar sectors requiring similar skills. In the Chinese auto industry, foreign producers offer unskilled line workers more than twice the going rate for unskilled manufacturing jobs. Most also offer more benefits, such as health insurance, transportation, and training. Real wages in Mexico's automotive-assembly companies, all of them foreign, have grown by more than 16 percent annually since 1990, from levels that were already far above the country's average manufacturing wages—greatly outstripping productivity growth. Foreign companies pay premium wages to attract the best employees, raise their motivation, and reduce turnover while still enjoying significant labor savings.

Companies that make export-oriented foreign direct investments pose little threat to domestic producers because the foreigners aren't competing for local market share. On the contrary, domestic companies often stand to gain as foreign ones look for local distributors and suppliers. They can also benefit by copying and building on the activities of the foreign competition, as domestic Chinese consumer electronics and high-tech companies and the formidable Indian outsourcing firms have done.

The folly of incentives

Governments around the world woo foreign direct investment by offering costly tax breaks, import duty exemptions, land and power subsidies, and other enticements. Yet our evidence suggests that they are largely ineffective.

In many cases, governments give away substantial sums for investments that would have been made anyway. India, for instance, waived its 35 percent tax on corporate profits for companies that moved back-office processing and IT jobs there—a concession worth roughly $6,000 annually for every full-time IT employee and $2,000 for every processing one. These measures, following similar concessions by the Philippines, might have been needed to offset perceived risk when the industry was in its infancy. But they are almost certainly irrelevant today when India commands more than a quarter of the global market. Our survey of 30 executives at companies that have moved jobs to India revealed that financial incentives were the least important factor in the decision (see "When money matters least"). Most of the executives told us that they would rather see the government spend its money upgrading the local infrastructure.

Executives of other multinational companies agree. Our interviews showed that the primary considerations when they invest abroad are the quality of the infrastructure and the labor force, the size and growth of the domestic market, and the accessibility of the location. In theory, if all else were equal, financial incentives might sway an investment decision. But all else is never equal, particularly when companies weigh the dozens of considerations factored into international investments.

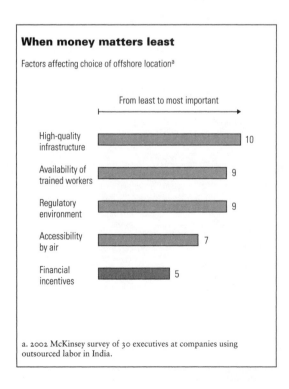

When money matters least

Factors affecting choice of offshore location[a]

From least to most important

High-quality infrastructure	10
Availability of trained workers	9
Regulatory environment	9
Accessibility by air	7
Financial incentives	5

a. 2002 McKinsey survey of 30 executives at companies using outsourced labor in India.

To make matters worse for state and municipal governments, they get into bidding wars to win particular investments—a competition every bit as common in rich countries, where such authorities vie for new auto plants (see "The winner's curse") and professional sports teams. Yet even in the case of these bidding wars, financial incentives often don't stand high on a company's list of considerations. Ford executives, for instance, say that the top three factors in their decision to build a plant in the Indian state of Tamil Nadu were the availability of a supplier

The winner's curse

Government-supplied investment incentives in automobile industry

Date of package	Country of project	Investor	Cost per job,[a] $
1980	United States	Honda	4,000
early 1980s	United States	Nissan	17,000
1984	United States	Mazda–Ford	14,000
mid-1980s	United States	GM Saturn	27,000
mid-1980s	United States	Mitsubishi–Chrysler	35,000
mid-1980s	United States	Toyota	50,000
mid-1980s	United States	Fuji–Isuzu[b]	51,000
early 1990s	United States	Mercedes-Benz	168,000
1992	Portugal	Ford–Volkswagen	265,000
1995	Brazil	Volkswagen	54,000–94,000
1996	Brazil	Renault	133,000
1996	Brazil	Mercedes-Benz	340,000
1997	Germany	Volkswagen	180,000
1997	India	Ford	200,000–420,000

a. Estimated value of fiscal and financial incentives supplied by state and municipal governments to particular investment project divided by number of jobs project was expected to create directly.

b. Maker of Subaru.

Source: Charles P. Oman, *Policy Competition for Foreign Direct Investment: A Study of Competition among Governments to Attract FDI*, Organisation for Economic Co-operation and Development, 1999.

base and skilled labor as well as the quality of the infrastructure.[2] The generous financial incentives Ford received were only as important as proximity to a port. Land subsidies were even less significant.

When incentives do attract foreign investment, unintended consequences often follow. Fiscal costs can escalate as incentives are extended to local companies. Furthermore, generous incentives can encourage too much investment, as they did in Brazil's automotive industry. Responding to subsidies worth more than $100,000 for each job created, foreign carmakers added 40 percent more capacity, we estimate, than would otherwise have been built during the late 1990s. By 2002, the industry was saddled with 80 percent overcapacity. Low utilization rates have eroded the productivity of domestic and foreign players by at least 20 percent and tied up capital that could have been used more efficiently elsewhere in the economy.

Sometimes, incentives subsidize inefficient production that wouldn't exist without them. Brazil's government, for example, tried to get consumer electronics companies, foreign and domestic, to locate in Manaus by offering tax incentives that cost it $576 million in 2001 alone. Manaus is in the middle of the Amazon, 2,500 miles from São Paulo and 500 miles upriver from the port of Belém. More than two months are needed to ship components from Asia and 10 to 20 days to move assembled products to São Paulo. Freight charges add 5 percent to production costs, and extra inventory adds at least 2 percent more. Skilled labor is often imported, negating any labor cost advantage. Only with breaks from the hefty taxes and tariffs imposed on production in Brazil could Manaus have attracted plants to produce goods in such an expensive, inconvenient location.

Regulations for foreign direct investment don't work

Even as governments in emerging markets dole out such lucrative incentives, many of these governments restrict the way foreign companies operate in order to protect local industry and to maximize spillovers to the domestic economy. The most popular restrictions are local-content requirements, which force foreign companies to purchase a certain percentage of inputs locally, and joint-venture requirements. Although local-content requirements are now illegal under World Trade Organization rules, developing countries find barriers—generally tariffs on components—to restrict the way companies operate. Our research casts doubt on the effectiveness of such measures. In most cases, they aren't needed to develop a supplier industry or to help local companies learn from foreign ones. In the few cases when they appear to work, they come at a high cost to the economy.

Local-content requirements existed in three of the industries we studied: automotive in India and China and consumer electronics in Brazil. Their overall economic impact was marginal at best. Interviews with executives of foreign carmakers in India, for instance, show that they would have sourced many components locally without local-content requirements. Why? Because of the cost and time required to import parts, the rapid escalation of import prices after the rupee lost value in 1991, and the large supply of relatively low-wage, technically trained workers in the local component industry. The same reasons likely apply to China's auto industry.

Our research clearly shows that local-content requirements aren't needed to develop a strong supplier industry. China doesn't have local-content requirements for consumer electronics, but its companies are rapidly moving from assembling final goods to producing the full value chain of components, all the way to semiconductors. This evolution has created a virtuous cycle of "crowding in" even more global players. Similarly, Mexico began phasing out local-content requirements for automakers in 1994 but still has seven times more jobs in companies that make components (which are also exported) than in final-assembly plants.

Local-content requirements may at times have increased the proportion of local components in finished goods, but only by shielding inefficient and subscale suppliers, lowering productivity, and raising prices for manufacturers and consumers. Consider the local-content requirements for consumer electronics made in Manaus. When they began to be phased out, in 1991, the proportion of foreign-made components went from less than 20 percent of the total (by value) in 1990 to more than 50 percent by 1995. We estimate that half of the local component makers in Manaus closed shop when faced with competition from imports. Consumers paid the price for all that inefficiency. The evidence about local-content requirements in our automotive cases points in the same direction. Although China is known for its low-cost manufacturing, local-content regulations for auto parts have not only increased their price but also made cars produced there 20 to 30 percent more expensive than cars produced in the United States. In India, we estimate, such regulations add 20 percent to the cost of cars.

We also found no compelling evidence to support the case for joint-venture requirements. When joint ventures make economic and strategic sense, foreign players pursue them. Neither Brazil nor Mexico has joint-venture requirements in retailing, but joint ventures were the most common way for foreign companies to enter those markets.[3] Local-market knowledge, after all, is crucial to success in service industries. In a low-margin business such as retailing, understanding the nuances of consumer preferences and building reliable local supply and distribution networks make the difference between success and failure, and foreign players operate at a disadvantage in these respects. In China and India, local partnerships often give foreign players the government contacts they need to cut through red tape.

More important, joint ventures, required or not, are hardly necessary for local companies to benefit from the presence of foreign ones. The fast-growing Indian vendors that provide back-office services to foreign companies got a start only after multinationals pioneered this approach—and trained a critical mass of local employees. (The CEO of Wipro Spectramind, for instance, started out at GE Capital, and the CEO of Daksh came from Motorola.) In Mexico, foreign carmakers introduced dealer financing decades ago—the beginnings of consumer financing there. (It has since spread to many industries.) Chinese consumer electronics and IT companies, such as Haier and Legend, are honing their skills by competing with foreign companies in China. Some, including Legend, have learned marketing and distribution techniques by serving as local distributors for global brands.

What really matters

To get the most from foreign direct investment, developing nations should abandon their incentives and regulations and concentrate instead on strengthening their economic foundations—in particular, stabilizing the economy and promoting competitive markets. Macroeconomic instability discourages long-term investment by making demand, prices, and interest rates difficult to forecast. Most foreign investment entered Brazil, for instance, only after the government stabilized its economy through the 1994 Real Plan.[4]

Competition is essential to diffuse the impact of foreign investment, for without competitive markets, the entry of foreign players has little effect on inefficient domestic incumbents and their productivity. Our only case study in which foreign direct investment failed to have a clearly positive impact dealt with banking in Brazil. A key reason was the industry's low competitive intensity: thanks to the high cost of switching banks and to entry barriers for new competitors, banking in any country is less competitive than other businesses. In Brazil this problem is exacerbated by high interest rates that make it more profitable to lend to the government than to consumers and by the lack of competition from nonbank players such as mutual funds.[5]

Foreign direct investment had the most dramatic positive impact when domestic incumbents—such as companies in Mexico's food-retailing industry, China's consumer electronics industry, and India's business-process outsourcing industry—weren't shielded from foreign rivals. To promote competitive markets, developing nations must reduce restrictions on foreign investment, lower import tariffs, streamline the requirements for starting new businesses, and encourage new market entrants.

Another important way of promoting fair competition is to crack down on companies in the informal economy (or "gray" market), which don't pay taxes or obey regulatory requirements. These dodges give such companies an unearned cost advantage, allowing them to stay in business despite their small scale and inefficiency. In the Brazilian food-retailing sector, for example, up to half of all companies are profitable because they underpay their value-added and payroll taxes. Similarly, small-scale (and often home-based) personal-computer-assembly companies in Brazil and India compete with leading global PC manufacturers by avoiding taxes that in some cases account for close to 50 percent of the consumer's final price. This lack of compliance not only robs government coffers but also allows informal players to maintain subscale and inefficient operations and thus impedes the transition to a more productive economy and a higher standard of living.

Finally, developing countries must continue to build a strong infrastructure, including roads, power supplies, and ports—particularly if they want to attract export-oriented foreign investment. In India, for instance, the continuing liberalization of the power and telecom sectors, a process that began in 1991, sparked an investment boom, which led to the upgrading of the infrastructure. That, in turn, became an important prerequisite for the development of the IT- and business-process outsourcing industry.

Increasingly, observers question whether globalization has broadly improved global standards of living. The evidence from our research shows clearly that it can and does. Rather than holding foreign direct investment at arm's length, developing nations should embrace it.

The authors wish to acknowledge the many MGI fellows who participated in the project underlying this article and the partners around the world who helped make the project possible:

Vivek Agrawal, Nelly Aguilera, Dino Asvaintra, Angelique Augereau, Vivek Bansal, Dan Devroye, Maggie Durant, Heinz-Peter Elstrodt, Antonio Farrini, Thomas-Anton Heinzl, Lan Kang, Ashish Kotecha, Martha Laboissière, Enrique Lopez, Maria McClay, Glenn Mercer, Gordon Orr, Vincent Palmade, Ranjit Pandit, Antonio Puron, Julio Rodriguez, Jaeson Rosenfeld, and Rodrigo Rubio.

Diana Farrell, Jaana K. Remes, and Heiner Schulz,
The McKinsey Quarterly, 2004 Number 1.

Notes

1. The full report, *New Horizons: Multinational Company Investment in Developing Economies,* is available free of charge at www.mckinsey.com/MGI.

2. R. Venkatesan, *Study on Policy Competition among States in India for Attracting Direct Investment,* New Delhi, India: National Council of Applied Economic Research, January 2000.

3. Of the three largest global retailers—Wal-Mart, Ahold, and Carrefour—Wal-Mart and Ahold primarily use joint ventures and acquisitions for international expansion. Carrefour uses greenfield investments and, to a lesser degree, joint ventures.

4. Earlier MGI research showed that partly because of recurring economic crises, Turkey receives little foreign direct investment given the size of its economy. See Didem Dincer Baser, Diana Farrell, and David E. Meen, "Turkey's quest for stable growth," *The McKinsey Quarterly,* 2003 special edition: *Global directions,* pp. 74–86 (www .mckinseyquarterly.com/links/10816).

5. The other reason for the failure of foreign direct investment to have a clearly positive impact on Brazil's banks was the fact that the best of them were already highly efficient, so the foreign competition had fewer opportunities to improve their performance.

6

Offshoring and beyond

Vivek Agrawal, Diana Farrell, and Jaana K. Remes

IDEAS IN BRIEF

Companies that simply export current operating models to low-wage economies in search of cost savings fail to realize the offshore environment's full potential to create value.

Offshoring companies could save more by reshaping each link in their value chain to take advantage of the very different ratio of labor to capital costs in low-wage offshore locations.

Significantly lower operating cost structures allow companies to grow their revenues by pursuing business ideas and entering new markets that would previously have been too costly to pursue.

The enticement to companies of a worker who earns $2 an hour in India as against ten times that amount for a worker in the United States is obvious. For years, such wage differentials have attracted leading manufacturing companies to low-wage nations. More recently, businesses of all kinds have also exported back-office functions such as data entry, payroll processing, and call centers. Business-process offshoring is all the rage, and the hundreds of companies that have taken this route often cut their costs by as much as half.

Yet as impressive as these achievements may appear, new research by the McKinsey Global Institute (MGI) finds that companies are leaving billions of dollars in savings behind when they offshore back-office functions and service jobs.[1] Such companies are merely replicating what they do at home, where labor is expensive and capital is relatively cheap, in countries in which the reverse is true. What is needed? Nothing less than a total transformation of business processes to harness the new environment's potential. And by undertaking such a transformation, many companies will find that the resulting lower cost structure releases massive new revenue opportunities even more valuable than the savings.

Halfway to global

The first wave of globalization began 100 or more years ago, when companies were lured abroad by the prospect of new markets. Even today, we estimate, the age-old motivation of reaching vast new customer pools explains perhaps 80 percent of cross-border investments. Many of them, such as Wal-Mart Stores' operations in Mexico and HSBC's in Malaysia, are in service sectors that require a local presence by definition. Others are in industries such as automotive, in which high tariffs and other trade barriers effectively force foreign companies to set up shop locally if they want to do business.

Despite the fits and starts of progress in world trade talks, the policy barriers that limit foreign investment and trade have fallen significantly over the past ten years. The result has been a second wave of globalization, in which companies from North America, Europe, and Japan build plants in low-wage countries to take advantage of enormous wage differentials and then export the finished goods back to the home market. These companies have substantially cut their costs for a variety of products, particularly labor-intensive ones such as textiles and toys, even taking into account the extra expense of transportation and overseas management and training.

Companies in a few industries have gone further, specializing in component production and final assembly in the countries or regions with the strongest comparative advantage. Nowhere is this third wave of globalization more evident than in consumer electronics (see "How far can it go?"). Business-process offshoring, made possible by the dramatic fall in telecommunications costs and the ability to transform paper-based activities into digital ones requiring only a telephone and a computer, is just the next logical step. A broad range of service jobs and back-office functions can now be performed remotely in India, for example, or in the Philippines. Low-skill work such as data entry and transaction processing, real-time customer support, and research services are obvious candidates. But even high-skill activities such as customized software development, the design of automotive and aerospace components (CAD/CAM), and pharmaceutical research are increasingly undertaken outside the United States.

Many of the jobs sent offshore may be considered undesirable and lacking in prestige in developed countries yet are highly attractive in developing ones. So offshore workers not only cost far less but also are often more highly motivated, which means that they perform better. One British bank's call-center agents in India, for instance, process 20 percent more transactions, with 3 percent more accuracy, than do their counterparts in the United Kingdom. Some companies set up their own "captive" operations in offshore locations to take advantage of these benefits, while others outsource to local companies, particularly in India.

Companies in the United States and Britain account for roughly 70 percent of the business-process offshoring market. Relatively liberal employment and labor laws give such companies flexibility in reassigning their activities and eliminating jobs, and they can take advantage of the sizable English-speaking populations in many low-wage countries, such as India, Ireland, the Philippines, and South Africa. With a shared language, errors are far less likely and functions that require voice interaction or text-based work are straightforward. The opportunities for continental European and Japanese companies are thus more limited.

Business-process offshoring is still a nascent industry. By our estimates, in 2002 it was worth $32 billion to $35 billion, just 1 percent of the $3 trillion worth of business functions that could be performed remotely. Because of the significant benefits already being realized through offshoring, the market is projected to grow by 30 to 40 percent annually over the next five years.[2]

This prospect may cause consternation over job losses in the United States, but it will make offshoring an industry with well over $100 billion in annual revenues by 2008.

Getting more from offshoring

Merely replicating processes developed at home, however, is not the way to realize offshoring's full potential. Wages represent 70 percent of call-center costs in the United States, for instance, so these operations are designed to minimize labor by using all available technology. But in low-wage India, that makes little sense, since wages represent only 30 percent of costs, and capital equipment (to provide telecom bandwidth, for example) is often more expensive than it is at home.

Pushing the envelope

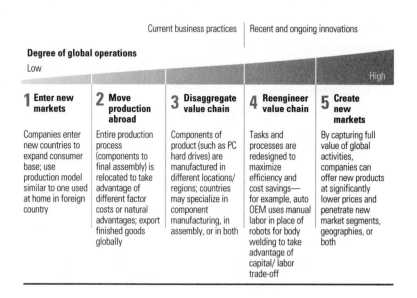

	Current business practices		Recent and ongoing innovations	
Degree of global operations Low → High				
1 Enter new markets	**2 Move production abroad**	**3 Disaggregate value chain**	**4 Reengineer value chain**	**5 Create new markets**
Companies enter new countries to expand consumer base; use production model similar to one used at home in foreign country	Entire production process (components to final assembly) is relocated to take advantage of different factor costs or natural advantages; export finished goods globally	Components of product (such as PC hard drives) are manufactured in different locations/ regions; countries may specialize in component manufacturing, in assembly, or in both	Tasks and processes are redesigned to maximize efficiency and cost savings— for example, auto OEM uses manual labor in place of robots for body welding to take advantage of capital/ labor trade-off	By capturing full value of global companies can offer new products at significantly lower prices and penetrate new market segments, geographies, or both

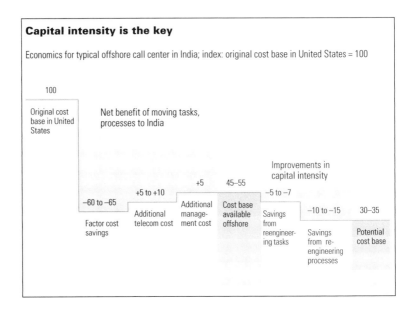

Capital intensity is the key

Economics for typical offshore call center in India; index: original cost base in United States = 100

The way to reduce the cost of offshore operations even further (see "Pushing the envelope") is to reorganize and reengineer operations to take full advantage of these differences. In a low-wage country, the capital infrastructure—including office space, telecommunications lines, and computer hardware and software—should be used as intensively as possible. For a call center, this approach can reduce costs by an additional 30 to 40 percent, boosting total savings to as much as 70 percent of the cost of on-shore operations (see "Capital intensity is the key"). The potential value for other offshored functions, like data entry, payroll processing, and financial accounting, is similar.

Companies can boost their capital productivity in low-wage environments in three ways:

- *Round-the-clock shifts.* The most obvious way to use the capital infrastructure more intensively is to run round-the-clock shifts, even if they mean higher wages for odd hours. This option simply wouldn't exist in a high-wage environment, where wage premiums offset any capital savings. We estimate that just by increasing the number of shifts, companies can reduce their operating costs by 30 to 44 percent for many types of offshore work, including financial accounting, procurement, call centers, transaction processing, and more complex functions such as knowledge services and R&D (see "Rock around the clock"). But in India, we found that even the most efficient third-party providers run only two shifts a day, and most of the captive operations set up by multinational corporations are running only one.

- *Cheaper capital equipment.* Some service providers in India are using cheap local labor to develop their own software instead of purchasing more expensive branded

Rock around the clock

Effects of additional shifts on operating costs, $ per billable seat per hour

Level of skills required ————————————————————————————————→

	Data entry, verification[a]			Rules-based decision making[a]			Knowledge-based services[a]		
	Fixed costs	Variable costs[b]	Total cost	Fixed costs	Variable costs[b]	Total cost	Fixed costs	Variable costs[b]	Total cost
Voice services[c]	7.8	4.0	11.8	7.8	4.6	12.4	7.8	6.8	14.6
	3.9	4.0	7.9	3.9	4.6	8.5	3.9	6.8	10.7
	2.6	4.0	6.6 −44%	2.6	4.6	7.2 −42%	2.6	6.8	9.4 −36%
Nonvoice services[c]	6.3	3.8	10.1	6.3	4.3	10.6	6.3	8.0	14.3
	3.1	3.8	6.9	3.1	4.3	7.4	3.1	8.0	11.1
	2.1	3.8	5.9 −42%	2.1	4.3	6.4 −40%	2.1	8.0	10.1 −30%

a. Data entry, verification include simple manual processes that don't require decision making; rules-based decision making includes services that don't require managerial judgment, can be performed with mechanical rules-based directions, and require minimal supervision; knowledge-based services require skilled, knowledge-based professionals such as engineers, MBAs, scientists.

b. Additional shifts in this example are daytime shifts and therefore require no wage premium

c. Voice services include multipurpose, multichannel interactions serving needs of many constituencies, including customers, distributors, employees, prospects, suppliers; nonvoice services include processing of back-office functions with turnaround time >4 hours.

products from the global software giants. American Express, for instance, hired programmers to write software to reconcile accounts, and the software now reconciles over three-quarters of them, or more than half a million every day. The company, which paid only $5,000 to develop this solution, estimates that licensing more sophisticated database software would have cost several million dollars. The Indian carmaker Maruti Udyog developed its own robots for its assembly lines; the robots, on average, cost a small fraction of what similar ones cost its partner Suzuki in Japan. In this way, companies maintain the level of automation that prevails in high-wage countries, but at a distinctly lower capital cost.

- *Reduced automation.* Some companies have gone a step further and used workers for tasks that would normally be automated at home. A payments processor, for example, might employ people to input checks manually into a computer system instead of using expensive imaging software. A telemarketing firm that would use expensive automatic dialers in a high-wage country might have workers make their own calls instead.

Manufacturers too can use this approach. Certain automotive original-equipment manufacturers (OEMs) in China use robots for only 30 percent of the welding in car assembly, as compared with 90 percent or more in US or European operations. (BMW's plant in South Africa employs the same line of attack.) In India, domestic car companies have reduced the need for automation throughout the manufacturing process: they use more manual labor to load and change dies in pressing, body welding, materials handling, and other functions—while suffering no discernible loss of quality in the finished product. In this way, these companies manage to cut their assembly costs by 4 to 5 percent or even more and save themselves millions of dollars annually.

Ultimately, companies might completely redesign the sequence in which tasks are performed, in order to leverage the opportunities above more fully. Consider the simple example of a call-center agent who manages customer accounts. In high-wage countries, each customer call is routed to an agent who listens to the request, opens up a computer database, and updates the account in real time. Neither the computer nor the telephone is used efficiently, since the agent is either talking or typing but not both.

Offshore, an agent equipped with only a telephone could write the customer request by hand into a tracking log and move on to the next call. Telecom costs are reduced because the agent spends less time on calls and customers less time on hold. Another agent, working at a computer station used around the clock, could enter the information into the database. While the new process requires more agents to handle requests, expensive computer hardware and software and telephone lines are used more intensively. Added wages are more than offset by savings on computers, software licenses, and telephone connections (see "Process reengineering lowers costs"). The economics of an Indian call center suggest that this simple change could actually boost current profit margins for offshoring vendors by as much as 50 percent.

Reengineering offshore functions makes sense only if wages stay low. Over time, they will rise and technology costs will continue to fall. As this happens, companies can adjust their operations to reflect changing factor costs. But in most low-wage

---

Process reengineering lowers costs

Change in operating costs for typical call center in India,[a] $ per billable seat per hour

Decrease in labor productivity		Cost of increased transaction-processing time and additional labor	+$1.20
Increase in capital productivity	Process reengineering	Savings from increased capital intensity (more efficient use of computers, telephones)	−$2.60
	Task reengineering	Savings from reduced software-licensing costs	−$0.20
		Net effect on operating costs	**−$1.60**

a. In this example, agent equipped with only a telephone writes customer requests by hand into tracking log; agent spends less time per call, customers spend less time on hold; second agent working second or third shift enters information into database.

---

countries, labor is so cheap and the labor pool so large that rising wages are unlikely to be a problem for decades. India each year produces 2 million college graduates—more than 80 percent of them English speakers—while China produces 850,000, though with minimal English skills. Even a small country like the Philippines annually produces 290,000 college graduates, all English speakers.

Beyond cost savings

By reaping offshoring's full potential, companies will find that their new, lower-cost structures open up a variety of opportunities to boost revenue growth. These opportunities will often far exceed the annual cost savings.

Some companies, for instance, can now chase delinquent accounts receivable they formerly had to ignore: one airline carrier is capturing $75 million in previously lost receivables on top of the $50 million it saves each year by operating its accounts-receivable department in India. Meanwhile, a leading US personal-computer manufacturer created telephone- and e-mail-based customer service centers in India to provide technical support. In addition to saving more than $100 million annually, it has significantly increased the proportion of customer problems it resolves. The company thereby reduces the number of follow-up calls it receives and the amount of merchandise it must replace while simultaneously boosting its customer satisfaction levels. And a financial-services firm has extended to customers with lower account balances services previously limited to high-net-worth clients, thus opening up large new customer segments in its home market.

The new cost position can also be used to develop cheaper products for consumers in emerging markets. Consider the experience of one of their own local companies. The Indian automaker Tata Motors (formerly Telco) designed the low-cost Indica car for the domestic market. The Indica sells for roughly 10 percent less than cars from global OEMs and breaks even on a volume of 150,000 units, a fraction of the number global companies need. That Indicas have fewer features accounts for a small part of the cost savings. Most of the savings come from a lower level of automation in assembly, a reengineered process, and the use of very-low-cost local labor to develop the car (at a quarter of what a global OEM would have spent to develop something similar). As a result, the company has grown from virtually nothing to capture a quarter of the Indian market in its segment during the past four years—displacing Suzuki Motor, Hyundai, and other global brands—and is now under contract to export 100,000 Indicas to the United Kingdom and continental Europe.

As companies go further down the road to globalization, the potential to create new markets and redefine industries is enormous. Consider how the dramatic price reductions made possible by globalizing production have changed the market for televisions in the United States. Just 25 years ago, almost a quarter of US households had no color TV. Since then, prices have declined by roughly 40 percent in real terms. Now 98 percent of US households have at least one, and many families have three or more. At the new price point, color televisions have been transformed from luxury items into nearly disposable goods that most of the population considers a necessity. And as color TVs have proliferated, they have given rise to an industry that produces television content and television-based games worth more than $30 billion. Although the detractors of globalization fear that it has already gone too far, we believe that it has barely begun.

How far can it go?

The personal computer on your desk today may have been designed in Taiwan and assembled in Mexico, with memory chips from South Korea, a motherboard from China, and a hard drive from Thailand. Not surprisingly, the value of world trade in consumer electronics components and final goods is 180 percent of the value of industry sales each year, and the industry has been completely restructured. Many companies around the world are now specializing in quite narrow segments of the value chain—for example, as innovators and designers of goods, low-cost producers, specialized assemblers, or marketers and distributors.

Countries too are starting to specialize: Mexico and eastern Europe take advantage of their location to assemble goods destined for the United States and Europe, respectively, and China uses its huge labor pool to become a global base for low-cost manufacturing. Although companies have benefited from lower costs and consumers have enjoyed dramatically lower prices and more choice, few nonmanufacturing industries have moved so decisively.

Clearly, not every industry could go as far as consumer electronics along the road to globalization: steel, for instance, is heavy and bulky to transport, while services such as retailing, banking, and entertainment must of necessity remain largely local. The interplay between the physical nature of any industry, its organizational environment, and the legal, regulatory, and policy barriers to its globalization determines its potential for restructuring.

The barriers to globalization are real, and many may not come down. But as an experiment, we looked at how much value could be created in the automotive industry if they did. We found that it could capture a staggering $150 billion annually in cost savings and an additional $170 billion annually in new revenues—a combination that would boost industry revenues by more than 25 percent from current levels. What stands in the way of achieving this increase?

Most people think that the industry is already global, largely because of the popularity of foreign cars. Few realize that of the 55 million vehicles produced each year, more than 90 percent are sold where they are made. Although the leading OEMs have all built plants in low-wage countries, these facilities were built to meet local or regional demand. Very few cars move from one geographic region to another, and until very recently only about 100,000 cars produced in low-wage countries were subsequently exported to high-wage ones.[a]

Yet there are few good reasons for this pattern. After all, it costs only $500 and takes only three weeks to ship an automobile anywhere in the world, and both the cost and the time are diminishing. More important, cars can be produced in low-wage countries for at least 20 percent less than in high-wage ones, even after shipping costs and tariffs are factored in (see "From India with love"). The resulting boon to the world's consumers could be enormous.

Furthermore, experience has shown that quality standards can be maintained in low-wage countries. BMW's South African plant, which exports to Europe and North America, is even slightly better than the German plant.[b] Volkswagen produces all of its popular New Beetles in Mexico. Operating in these countries often requires extra training for workers—BMW spends three to five times more on training in South Africa than it does in its other plants—but wage differences more than offset that cost.

Moreover, many analysts believe that overcapacity in the global automotive industry is now 30 percent or even higher. Much of the

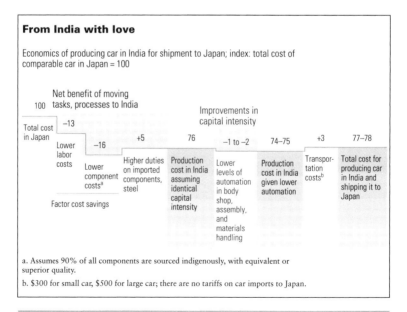

From India with love

Economics of producing car in India for shipment to Japan; index: total cost of comparable car in Japan = 100

Net benefit of moving tasks, processes to India

Improvements in capital intensity

100

Total cost in Japan −13

Lower labor costs −16

Lower component costs[a]

Factor cost savings

Higher duties on imported components, steel +5

Production cost in India assuming identical capital intensity 76

Lower levels of automation in body shop, assembly, and materials handling −1 to −2

Production cost in India given lower automation 74–75

Transportation costs[b] +3

Total cost for producing car in India and shipping it to Japan 77–78

a. Assumes 90% of all components are sourced indigenously, with equivalent or superior quality.

b. $300 for small car, $500 for large car; there are no tariffs on car imports to Japan.

overcapacity is in emerging markets, where governments granted lucrative incentives to global OEMs during the 1990s but local demand failed to materialize. These factories could be supplying developed countries with lower-cost cars. Confronted by idle plants in countries from Thailand to Brazil, a few OEMs are now moving in this direction.

The barriers to globalization are government policies and some of the industry's organizational features. Apart from Japan, virtually every country has car tariffs, which range from 2.5 percent in the United States to 10 percent in Europe and to over 100 percent in some developing countries. What's more, strong unions mount stiff resistance to moving production offshore. Many auto parts are proprietary and there is very little standardization across manufacturers. So the complex supply chain—which can include hundreds of direct suppliers, each relying on hundreds of subsuppliers—is still relatively fragmented despite current perceptions of rampant consolidation. And since assembly plants can cost up to half a billion dollars to build, OEMs have enormous sunk costs in their existing manufacturing facilities.

If the industry found ways to overcome these barriers, it could capture up to $320 billion annually in cost savings and new revenues. The first step would be to use existing plants in low-wage countries more efficiently. By cutting the current overcapacity in half, the industry could reap $10 billion annually.[c] By building all additional production capacity in low-wage countries, it could save a further $40 billion annually after five years. Over time, if OEMs migrated 70 percent of their assembly and components sourcing in high-wage countries to low-wage ones, they could realize savings in the neighborhood of $150 billion a year. (For most OEMs, as much as 30 percent of demand is variable and 70 percent stable and predictable. Moving 70 percent offshore is thus potentially feasible without making consumers wait longer to get their cars or building large inventories to compensate for fluctuating demand.)

But the benefits don't stop at cost savings. By taking advantage of low-cost labor and disaggregating supply chains, automakers could produce cars at least 20 to 25 percent more cheaply. If tariffs on parts were also to fall, these companies could, by conservative estimates, cut prices by 30 percent and unleash massive new demand. In emerging markets, where consumers are highly price sensitive and there is significant unmet demand for low-cost cars, we estimate that the industry could increase its sales by up to $100 billion a year.

In developed countries, where most consumers already own cars, cutting the price of the lowest-cost models by 30 percent (to $7,000, from $10,500) could produce roughly $70 billion in additional sales. Some of this demand would come from low-income households that currently don't own cars. But part of the opportunity would be generated by changing the way consumers view them: instead of having only one or two, households might opt for three or four, with some purchased just for fun. Parents might be more inclined to buy cars for their children, and young people might enter the market as well.

The potential value at stake in the auto industry is eye-popping but hardly unique. As the barriers to globalization continue to erode, many other industries could be restructured and capture similar value.

---

a. This estimate doesn't include production within the countries adhering to the North American Free Trade Agreement (NAFTA).

b. "Two-way street: Automakers get even more mileage from the Third World," *Wall Street Journal,* July 31, 2002.

c. For details on these calculations, see the October 2003 MGI report *New Horizons: Multinational Company Investment in Developing Economies,* available free of charge at www.mckinsey.com.

The authors would like to acknowledge the many MGI fellows who participated in the project and the partners around the world who helped make it possible: Nelly Aguilera, Dino Asvaintra, Angelique Augereau, Vivek Bansal, Dan Devroye,

Maggie Durant, Heinz-Peter Elstrodt, Antonio Farini, Thomas-Anton Heinzl, Lan Kang, Ashish Kotecha, Martha Laboissière, Enrique Lopez, Ramesh Mangaleswaran, Maria McClay, Glenn Mercer, Gordon Orr, Vincent Palmade, Ranjit Pandit, Antonio Puron, Julio Rodriguez, Jaeson Rosenfeld, Rodrigo Rubio, and Heiner Schulz. We also wish to acknowledge members of the McKinsey initiative on business-process outsourcing and offshoring, including Detlev Hoch, Noshir Kaka, Anil Kumar, Sunish Sharma, Stefan Spang, Sanoke Viswanathan, and Patrick Woetzel. Their work contributed significantly to our understanding of the software- and business-process offshoring sectors.

Vivek Agrawal, Diana Farrell, and Jaana K. Remes,
The McKinsey Quarterly, 2003 Special Edition: *Global directions.*

Notes

1. See the October 2003 MGI report *New Horizons: Multinational Company Investment in Developing Economies,* available free of charge at www.mckinsey.com. During the yearlong research project leading up to this report, we conducted in-depth case studies of foreign direct investment in five sectors (automotive, consumer electronics, retail banking, retailing, and the offshoring of information technology and business processes) in four major developing economies (Brazil, China, India, and Mexico). These cases generated the basis of our findings and conclusions.

2. Consensus estimates of the market research firms Aberdeen Group, Gartner, and IDC.

7

Smarter offshoring

Diana Farrell

IDEAS IN BRIEF

During the past 15 years, companies have flocked to a handful of cities in India and Eastern Europe for offshore service functions.

Demand for young professionals is outstripping supply, wages and turnover are soaring, and overburdened infrastructure systems are struggling to serve the explosive growth.

More than 90 percent of the vast and rapidly growing pool of university-educated people suitable for work in multinationals is located outside the current hot spot cities.

In choosing a location, companies will have to focus less on low wages and much more on other ways that candidate cities can fulfill their business needs.

Companies will have to be much more rigorous in articulating precisely what they require from an offshore location, which means evaluating their unique needs on a range of dimensions and understanding how alternative locations can meet those needs for the foreseeable future.

The practice of moving service jobs to low-wage countries is entering a new phase. For offshoring functions ranging from computer programming and R&D to call-center and back-office tasks, US and western European companies will have to expand substantially the number of locations they consider. In choosing a city, they will have to focus less on low wages and much more on other ways that candidate cities can fulfill their business needs.

In the past ten to 15 years, the vast majority of offshore service jobs have gone to just a handful of cities in India, Eastern Europe, and Russia, notably Hyderabad, Bangalore, Delhi, Mumbai, Budapest, Prague, and Moscow. But popularity has come at a price. The turnover rate among IT staff in the banking industry is 30 percent to 40 percent in some Indian cities, and hiring graduates from the country's prestigious technology institutes has become a nightmare. "You have to wait in line from 5 a.m. and make commitments to applicants on the spot," reports a recruiter who has been hunting for engineers to fill posts in packaged-software and IT hardware companies.

In Mumbai, a hot spot for overseas investment banks, escalating wages and accelerating turnover are beginning to worry firms that need college graduates for sophisticated jobs such as reconciling foreign-exchange transactions. In Bangalore, the demand for college-educated people fluent in English to staff offshore call centers has pushed wages up. The story is similar in Moscow and St. Petersburg, where pay for software engineers has soared by 50 percent in the past two to three years. Prague seems to be heading down the same path. We project that its local colleges and universities will be hard-pressed to meet the demand for IT engineers by 2008.

Little wonder that some executives are questioning whether the touted endless supply of low-cost talent in developing countries is already drying up. The happy answer is that the tight labor markets in the hot spots are the exception, not the rule.

The McKinsey Global Institute (MGI) recently assessed the supply of college graduates suitable for employment by multinational companies in 28 low-wage countries. We found that there is a huge and rapidly growing pool of low-wage talent dispersed around the globe. (See "The vast talent pool.") More than 90 percent of these

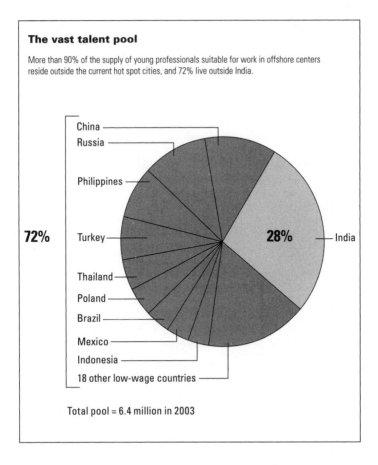

The vast talent pool

More than 90% of the supply of young professionals suitable for work in offshore centers reside outside the current hot spot cities, and 72% live outside India.

72%

China
Russia
Philippines
Turkey
Thailand
Poland
Brazil
Mexico
Indonesia
18 other low-wage countries

28%
India

Total pool = 6.4 million in 2003

people are located outside the current hot spots. Some live in countries with offshoring hubs but in less well-known cities—for instance, Zlin in the Czech Republic and the so-called third-tier Indian cities such as Ahmedabad and Chandigarh. Some are ready and waiting in countries that are just entering the fray—South Africa, Morocco, Argentina, and Brazil, among others. Pioneers such as Amazon.com, Telefónica, Intel, and Sakonnet Technology have recently established or announced plans for offshore centers in Cape Town, Tangier, Córdoba, and Rio de Janeiro, respectively.

Not all companies will feel comfortable locating an offshore operation—especially their first—somewhere that's not tried-and-true. But to make a rational choice, they need to compare the real costs of treading the well-worn path with those of going somewhere new. That means evaluating their unique needs for a given offshore operation along several dimensions (such as skill level of workers, connectivity, and the business environment) and understanding how various locations can meet those needs—and at what risk and cost—for the foreseeable future.

Most companies today don't take that approach. Even those with sophisticated international networks usually consider only a few locations on the basis of their previous experience and what other companies are doing. Most also use a fairly narrow set of decision criteria, with labor costs, time-zone considerations, and creature comforts generally paramount. To make the right choice among the increasing number of possible locations, these companies must consider other important factors such as wage-inflation trends, future labor supplies, and recruitment costs.

Why companies hunt in packs

The offshoring pioneers in the early 1990s—global giants like General Electric and British Airways—were drawn to locations with excellent universities that offered plentiful supplies of first-rate talent at low wages. After seeing these first movers' cost advantages, other companies began flocking to the same cities. Local service vendors cropped up, offering homegrown alternatives to captive centers. All this activity encouraged public and private investment in local infrastructure, and business and living environments improved. The clusters also promoted the easy exchange of ideas and people between businesses and local universities. Over time, some clusters developed talent pools with distinctive skills, making them all but irresistible to companies that valued those skills. Once those dynamics were set in motion, the risks for followers continued to fall.

But there is a tipping point. When too many companies pile into a city too fast, not only does its labor market overheat but it often cannot expand its infrastructure fast enough to serve the explosive growth in demand. Consider Gurgaon, a suburb of New Delhi, which has attracted numerous foreign companies, including Fidelity Investments, Nokia, and Microsoft. Construction has boomed: a half-dozen shopping malls have sprung up, and some three dozen more are in the works. But Gurgaon's paralyzing traffic congestion, frequent power outages, and communications blackouts make it difficult for residents to live comfortably, let alone work efficiently.

Companies with operations in cities with rising costs and deteriorating working conditions are understandably reluctant to pull out because of their sunk costs. This is particularly true for capital-intensive operations such as call centers or R&D facilities. (Setting up a typical 250-seat call center, for instance, costs $5.2 million.) The inherent "stickiness" of established offshore locations makes it crucial to choose the right one the first time. Accordingly, a company planning an operation offshore should at least consider the many attractive alternatives to the hot spots.

Beyond the hot spots

In the 28 low-wage countries that MGI studied, there were about 6.4 million young professionals suitable for offshore jobs in 2003. "Suitable" professionals are university graduates with up to seven years of experience who have the skills and attributes (language skills, technical knowledge, ability to interact successfully in a corporate environment) that multinationals want. Although not all these workers live in or near a major city, we believe that multinationals could gain access to the majority of them.

The percentage of suitable professionals varies widely from country to country. For instance, 10 percent of engineers in China are suitable for employment in a multinational, compared with 20 percent of Filipino engineers. So even though China's population is 16 times the size of the Philippines', its pool of suitable engineers is only three times as big. Likewise, Poland has nearly as many suitable engineers as Russia, which is much more populous.

MGI projects that the supply of college-educated talent will continue to outstrip the demand from multinationals' offshore operations for many years to come in nearly all of the eight occupational categories we analyzed. For instance, we project that the supplies of support staff and young professional generalists suitable for employment by multinational companies in emerging markets will exceed demand by 98 percent and 78 percent, respectively, in 2008. Only the aggregate supply of engineers in low-wage countries looks as though it will be a little tight. (See "The supply and demand outlook.")

The bright outlook for the overall supply of low-wage talent is due in large part to the robust growth in the number of university graduates that developing countries are churning out: 5.5 percent

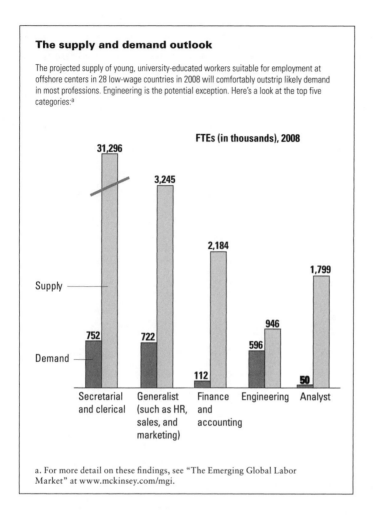

The supply and demand outlook

The projected supply of young, university-educated workers suitable for employment at offshore centers in 28 low-wage countries in 2008 will comfortably outstrip likely demand in most professions. Engineering is the potential exception. Here's a look at the top five categories:[a]

FTEs (in thousands), 2008

	Secretarial and clerical	Generalist (such as HR, sales, and marketing)	Finance and accounting	Engineering	Analyst
Supply	31,296	3,245	2,184	946	1,799
Demand	752	722	112	596	50

a. For more detail on these findings, see "The Emerging Global Labor Market" at www.mckinsey.com/mgi.

per year, compared with an annual increase of just 1 percent in developed countries. Of course, developed countries have a larger base of graduates, but faster growth in the developing world's graduate pool is closing the gap.

For instance, in 2003, there were about 30 percent fewer engineers in low-wage economies than in high- and mid-wage countries. By 2008, when young professional engineers worldwide will number more than 2 million, that gap will be 18 percent. The supply of suitable finance and accounting professionals from developing countries will outnumber those from high-wage ones by that time. Growth in the supply of graduates with qualifications that multinationals most desire is particularly rapid: in just five years, the proportion of degrees awarded in business and economics has jumped from 18 to 31 percent of the total in Russia and from 16 to 36 percent of the total in Poland.

The huge aggregate supply of competent professionals available for hire in emerging markets means that their average wages will remain relatively low for the foreseeable future, despite what the current wage inflation in offshore hot spots might suggest. Consider engineers, the most supply-constrained occupational category. Our model indicates that when aggregate demand pushes up wages for engineers in India (where average pay is the lowest in the world) from the current 12 percent of US levels to about 30 percent, companies will begin to employ graduates from the many other countries—including the Philippines, China, and Mexico—where average wages will be lower or comparable. Because the supply of engineers from these countries will be sufficient to satisfy all likely demand from companies' offshore operations until at least 2015, as far as we can reasonably project, we believe that the average wages for engineers in all these countries will not rise above the 30 percent mark.

At the same time, offshoring is unlikely to cause wages in high-wage countries to decrease significantly. (The only exceptions will be a few niche occupations such as low-value-added software coding.) That's because total offshore employment in services will likely represent a tiny fraction of overall employment in developed economies for decades. These trends indicate that offshoring will be a strategy worth pursuing for many years.

Emerging new candidates

Even within countries that already attract a lot of offshore operations, there are untapped pools of qualified and less expensive labor beyond the hot spots. Managers can find these people if they use their imaginations. In some instances, companies may be able to persuade attractive employees to move from other cities to their hot spot operations—for example, with low-cost, preapproved loans for housing. Managers of the larger offshore centers in Prague have used such tactics to recruit from other Czech and Slovakian cities like Brno and Bratislava. Similar tactics might also be appropriate in China. Only about one-quarter of graduates in China live in a city or region that's close to a major international airport and, therefore, is a viable place for an offshore operation. But MGI's analysis of migration patterns indicates that some 34 percent of Chinese graduates in the less accessible areas would be willing to move for a good job. (In contrast, in Russia, where one-third of graduates live near a major airport, only 16 percent of the rest would be prepared to move nearer to one for the sake of a job.)

Setting up operations in towns that are within a reasonable drive of a major airport or arranging for employees to telecommute are other ways to reach untapped pools of talent. Companies are employing both approaches in India, for example. Several companies that now find Mumbai overheated have established smaller operations in the (for now) pleasant university town of Pune, 120 miles away. Some IT operations, both local vendors and captive offshore ventures, have begun to employ telecommuters in cities such as Chandigarh and Mysore for simple tasks such as typing, data entry, and order processing.

For their part, governments in a number of low-wage nations are assessing what distinctive advantages their countries offer (in terms of labor skills, risk profile, or communications infrastructure, for example) and are targeting multinationals most likely to appreciate those advantages.

Dubai, for instance, is a relative newcomer to the global labor market. Its government sponsored a study of the strengths and weaknesses of rival offshore locations to identify a niche where it might outperform them. The study found Dubai's disadvantages—fairly high labor and telecommunications costs and the tiny sales potential of its local market compared with, say, China—are offset to an extent by its multinational, skilled, and stable workforce (Dubai law forbids frequent job changes); robust infrastructure; zero taxes; and five-star amenities. Dubai is now marketing itself as the ideal location for IT disaster recovery and backup facilities for companies with IT-intensive offshore operations in countries like India and the Philippines, where labor is cheaper but the infrastructure is also less robust.

South Africa offers a package that it believes is particularly attractive to companies in the insurance and banking sectors: a pool of qualified people (the country has an unusually large number of actuaries), a well-developed telecommunications and IT infrastructure, and good business services. South Africa does not match India on cost—a call-center seat in Cape Town costs one-third more to operate (although still about half what it would cost in the United Kingdom). Moreover, telecommunications are more expensive than in competitor countries, and the inherent risks of doing business in South Africa are relatively high. Still, South African employees prize call-center jobs—unlike some employees in central European cities—and are thus highly motivated and disinclined to hop from job to job. South Africa also boasts certain skills advantages. For instance, some British insurers recognize South African accreditation for claims processors. So even though the country might look unappealing on the basis of costs alone, those that give more weight to its other benefits will find it highly attractive. Amazon.com opened a software development center in Cape Town in 2005, and IBM has plans for a call center in Johannesburg for corporate clients.

Other countries are positioning themselves to multinationals with some success. Morocco is now home to customer-care and back-office processing centers that perform work for a number of major French and Spanish companies requiring fluent speakers of their home languages. Neighboring Tunisia has used its stable, low-cost workforce, modern infrastructure, and business-friendly regulations to attract companies such as Siemens, GE Capital Bank, and Wanadoo, the Internet service provider. Vietnam offers university graduates who are well schooled in mathematics, speak French, English, German, or Russian, and don't demand high wages. (They expect a starting salary only a little higher than that of unskilled factory workers in China.) Attracted by these advantages, World'Vest Base, a Chicago-based company that provides market data to investors around the globe, employs about 50 young, mostly female graduates in Ho Chi Minh City to search for information on the Web.

Navigating the global labor market

The problems facing the hot spots, coupled with the emergence of many more countries able and willing to provide offshore services, mean that picking a site has become more complicated. A company needs a process for articulating precisely what it requires from an offshore location and assessing all the locations that could meet those needs into the future at acceptable cost and risk. This involves evaluating current conditions and how dynamic supply and demand conditions in the local labor markets are likely to affect the company's operation over time. (See "Factors in choosing a location.")

A company should weight data on alternative sites on the basis of the relative importance of the factors driving its decision to go offshore. If the need for the lowest-cost talent is the main impetus, then data on this factor should receive the highest weighting. But many companies will want to give substantial weight to other factors, such as the size of the market accessible from a particular site or whether any managers from the home country will want to live there. The outcome of this process is a simple ranking of potential locations based on a much more granular understanding of their relative attractions than companies may have today. (See "Comparing locations objectively.")

This kind of rigorous approach is important not just for companies establishing their first captive offshore operation. Firms adding new captive operations to those they already own as well as companies taking the vendor route—that is, outsourcing a function or process to an independent offshore provider—will also benefit from such an analysis.

A company that already has an extensive global network of captive operations may understandably feel justified in locating a new operation somewhere it already knows, without further analysis. Using existing management resources, infrastructure, and government connections in a familiar place obviously lessens the risk of any new venture overseas. But the familiar may not necessarily be best for the business. One packaged-software company based in the United States had a strong bias toward locating an offshore center in India. It had sales operations there, and many of its board members were Indian. A rigorous, objective analysis of potential locations, however, showed that a service center located in a city in China had a markedly higher net present value than one in India. The reason: the center would help the company gain access to the appreciably larger domestic Chinese market by providing valuable local knowledge, contacts, and managerial expertise.

Similarly, Intel decided last November to open its next overseas software-development center in Córdoba, Argentina, rather than simply expand existing software-development centers in China and Russia. Intel said Argentina's strategic plan for nurturing its software industry, which includes tax breaks for technology companies and increased investments in education and research, influenced its choice.

Companies choosing to outsource to local vendors may feel their time would be better spent analyzing the terms of offers from competing vendors rather than weighing the pros and cons of competing locations. But unless a company understands the dynamics of the locations where vendors operate, it won't be able to understand whether the vendors will be able to meet the company's needs for any length of time. Where it's possible to switch vendors easily, this may be less of a consideration. But switching vendors also involves extra costs and a lot of management attention.

A global financial-services company employed such an approach in picking an offshore vendor to perform its back-office finance and accounting processes. Its board of directors had a strong preference for using a vendor in India. However, the company decided to consider other vendors and analyzed a number of locations in India, eastern Europe, and Asia. Knowing the circumstances of the labor market in various cities meant the management team could ask competing vendors detailed questions about their plans for handling wage increases or turnover should their labor markets heat up. For example, did a vendor have contingency plans to open new locations in the same country or move to a city in a different country? Was it planning to expand the potential labor supply by training less-qualified staff in-house? This line of questioning led the company to select a candidate that had most of its operations in an eastern European city and backup services in Asia.

A process for choosing sites that is deeply rooted in a company's unique business needs will lead different companies to make different choices. In many cases, such an approach may result in decisions that are counterintuitive or defy original assumptions.

For the very risk averse, a known hot spot may be the most rational location for a major new operation. Consider the recent decision of a midsize regional bank to establish a captive offshore center that will employ 1,500 information technology professionals in an Indian hot spot. Despite the city's overheating labor market, the bank still ranked it number one of the ten locations it assessed. The bank knew the city: it had run an offshore center there that had employed a few hundred back-office people for the past ten years. Some major competitors had large operations in the area similar to the new one the bank wanted to establish, so the incoming bank knew it could recruit the skills it needed. The local climate and culture suited the bank's expatriate managers. There were direct flights to and from its home city. Finally, the bank's executives were confident that it would still reap a substantial cost advantage even if it had to pay considerably more down the road to attract and retain talent. (There is now an 80 percent difference between wages for software engineers in the bank's home country and those in the Indian city. But the executives calculated that even if wage inflation among Indian software engineers were to run rampant, there would still be a 40 percent gap in 20 years.) Costs in other locations were likely to remain lower for a long time, but because of the heavier weight that the bank gave to risk and other factors, the known hot spot won the contest.

Companies that are marginally less risk averse are likely to find a range of appealing alternatives to the hot spots even if cost is their major preoccupation. A North American airline seeking a new location for its customer-support function ranked 16 cities in low- and high-wage countries on the basis of six criteria. The company gave a 40 percent weighting to costs in its decision, and cities in India and China were in first and second place on that measure alone. When all the criteria were taken into account, however, cities in several other countries were right behind those in India and China. Instead of outsourcing the operation to a vendor in India, the board's original intention, the location team is now leaning toward a vendor in Brazil because of its more attractive living environment and infrastructure.

Building a sustainable market

By giving more thought to how prospective offshore sites can serve their special needs and not just following the pack, companies stand to reap broader, longer-term advantages. One of these is lower labor costs in developing countries overall. The expansion of the offshore market to include many new cities will cause wage levels for young professionals to rise smoothly and gradually across emerging markets. Even the increases in the existing hot spots will be held in check.

US and western European companies will not be the only beneficiaries of these trends. Many cities and countries that have so far played only minor roles in the emerging global labor market will also benefit. Offshore operations will provide them with badly needed employment and capital. Entrepreneurial college graduates will have opportunities to develop the skills and management experience they need to start local businesses of their own that serve both foreign and local corporations. The result will be a growing middle class of professionals and accelerating economic growth that will help struggling countries raise themselves out of poverty. By casting their nets wider for low-wage talent, US and western European corporations can help these countries and themselves.

Factors in choosing a location

To make the right offshoring decisions, companies should assemble detailed information on a number of factors:

Cost

- Labor: current average wages for skilled workers and managers
- Infrastructure: unit costs for telecom networks, Internet access, and power
- Real estate: cost of class A office space
- Corporate taxes: the total tax burden or, conversely, the tax breaks and other incentives for local investment

Availability of skills

- Skill pool: size of labor force with the required skills
- Size of offshore sector: dollar volume and share of employment in the sector, as well as share of these services as a percentage of total exports
- Vendor landscape: size of local sector providing IT services and other business functions

Environment

- Government support: policy on foreign investment, labor laws, bureaucratic and regulatory burden, and level of corruption

- Business environment: compatibility with prevailing business culture and ethics
- Living environment: overall quality of life, prevalence of HIV infection, and serious crimes per capita
- Accessibility: travel time, flight frequency, and time difference

Market potential

- Attractiveness of local market: current GDP and GDP growth rate
- Access to nearby markets: in the host country and adjacent region

Risk profile

- Disruptive events: risk of labor uprising, political unrest, and natural disasters
- Security: risks to personal security and property from fraud, crime, and terrorism
- Regulatory risk: stability, fairness, and efficiency of legal framework
- Macroeconomic risk: cost inflation, currency fluctuation, and capital freedom
- Intellectual-property risk: strength of data and IP protection regime

Quality of infrastructure

- Telecom and IT: network downtime, speed of service restoration, connectivity
- Real estate: availability and quality
- Transportation: scale and quality of road and rail network
- Power: reliability of power supply

Comparing locations objectively

The McKinsey Global Institute's approach to comparing potential offshore locations can help executives make decisions on the basis of facts rather than intuition, personal preferences, or past experience. Not every company will have the resources to gather all the detailed data we recommend. That's okay. What matters more is gathering enough data to gain an understanding of the strengths and weaknesses of potential locations.

1. Draw up a long list of possible locations.

All companies will have some high-level reasons for pursuing an offshore venture—the need to reduce costs, find new sources of revenue, or secure new sources of talent, for instance. They will also have some general aversions—for example, they might not like the idea of locating a new venture in a distant time zone or in a country known for political instability. With considerations like these in mind, a company can draw up a list of eight or so candidate cities in three to five countries.

2. Define the decision criteria.

Our research shows that companies typically use six key factors to describe their ideal offshore location: the overall cost of operating; the availability of the skills they seek; the sales potential of the national domestic market and adjacent markets; the intrinsic risk of doing business in the location; the attractiveness of the business and living environments; and the quality of the infrastructure. In winnowing down the locations on its long list, a company will need to consider a number of subcriteria. For example, the overall quality of a city's infrastructure depends on the reliability of the telecommunications network and power supply, the availability of good office space, and the state of the roads and railways.

3. Collect data for each potential location.

Some data will be quantitative, such as labor costs for the various skill levels the company requires. Some will be more qualitative, such as assessments of risk. But a company can make objective assessments, even for qualitative criteria, by consulting the right information sources. In assessing a location's risk, for example, possible sources of information including the Economist Intelligence Unit's industrial-relations rating, the World Competitiveness Yearbook's personal security and private property index, and the United Nations Development Program's disaster risk index table.

Some data, such as the potential of the domestic market, will apply to all places in the country. But in many instances, the information can vary significantly across cities, including those in the same country. What are the local costs of labor, telecommunications, power, and real estate? How high are local business taxes? Is the city prone to flooding?

Managers then give the location a score (say, on a scale from 1 to 5) on each factor.

4. Give more weight to the criteria that matter most to your company.

Companies should assign weights to all criteria so that the final score reflects their relative importance. A bank based in Europe that was keen to enter new, large markets gave its highest weighting to criteria measuring market potential, for example, while a U.S. financial institution that was looking for a location for a captive IT center to serve its U.S. customers gave highest weightings to cost, infrastructure, and risk, particularly security.

Assigning appropriate weightings to each criterion is a subjective task. But that's a strength of the approach: the discussion allows managers to reach a shared understanding of those factors that will maximize revenue, minimize cost, or both for the activity in question.

That is a discussion management teams need to have, even if they don't do all the detailed math.

5. Rank locations in order of their attractiveness to your company.

The next step is to multiply the scores by their weightings and then average the weighted scores to arrive at an overall score for each location under consideration. Now the site-selection team can identify the two or three cities that may qualify as the best locations.

6. Assess the dynamics of the labor pool.

The final test for the short-listed cities is whether the local talent supply is sustainable. Companies must estimate future supply and demand for young professionals and middle managers in the occupations the company is most likely to recruit locally. Using data from local colleges and interviews with HR executives who know the city, companies can come up with a rough estimate of how many young people will graduate from local schools over the next five years or so in the relevant disciplines, what fraction are likely to fit into a multinational environment, and how easy it will be to fill any gaps with graduates from other cities in the same country. Other companies' plans to extend or build new offshore centers in the city will give a picture of growth in future demand. Examining recent movements in wage levels and turnover rates will show whether the local labor supply in any particular skill area is already constrained. This information will also help companies make educated guesses about how long current wage levels are likely to last in the occupations of interest.

Harvard Business Review, June 2006.

8

US offshoring: rethinking the response

Diana Farrell and Jaeson Rosenfeld

IDEAS IN BRIEF

Protectionism is the wrong response to offshoring.

Contrary to popular opinion, only 11 percent of US jobs could be feasibly offshored, and only a small fraction of these actually will be.

The impact of offshoring on US wages is imperceptible and its effects on employment are very small compared with normal job turnover in the economy.

Maintaining open polices on trade is essential if the United States is to continue to enjoy not only the benefits of offshoring but also the inflow of foreign direct investment it receives—the highest in the world—and its substantial trade surplus in services.

US reemployment assistance programs, however, should be expanded to ease the transition for those Americans whose jobs are eliminated by offshoring.

Companies from the United States lead the world in offshoring white-collar jobs to low-wage countries. Today they employ more than 900,000 offshore service workers, doing everything from developing software to answering customers' questions and conducting R&D. By 2008, US companies are expected to employ more than 2.3 million offshore service workers (See "Trend in worldwide offshore labor, 2003–2008"). *Foreign Affairs* magazine's recent poll of US public opinion finds widespread concern about the effects on the US job market.[1] Some policy makers have responded by calling for legislation to limit offshoring and a few states have already adopted such legislation.

Trying to protect jobs this way is a mistake. New research by

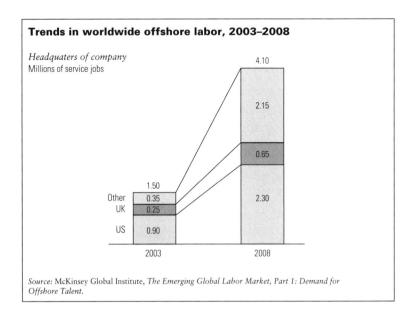

Trends in worldwide offshore labor, 2003–2008

Headquaters of company
Millions of service jobs

Source: McKinsey Global Institute, *The Emerging Global Labor Market, Part 1: Demand for Offshore Talent.*

the McKinsey Global Institute shows that many fewer jobs can be performed remotely than is commonly presumed.[2] For the United States, no more than several hundred thousand jobs per year will be lost to offshoring. That is far fewer than the normal rate of job turnover in the economy: 4.7 million Americans started jobs with a new employer in the single month of May 2005.[3] Because of this limited scale, the impact of offshoring on wage levels will also be negligible.

Preventing companies from offshoring will deprive high-wage economies of the multiple benefits it confers. Savings from offshoring allow companies to invest in next-generation technologies, creating jobs at home as well as abroad. Global competition sharpens companies' skills: US software makers improve their performance by competing with China, just as call centers do through competition with India. And refusing to buy services provided overseas will invite retaliation. Since it runs a trade *surplus* in services and leads the world in attracting inward foreign direct investment, the United States has the most to lose from a services trade war.

There is no doubt that maintaining an open market in services brings substantial benefits to developed economies (see "Is offshoring a harmful form of trade?").[4] But none of these benefits at present flow directly to those who undeniably suffer as a result—those workers whose jobs move overseas. This doesn't weaken the case for free trade; rather, it warrants a shift in the debate. Instead of trying to limit offshoring, we need to allocate the benefits from this new form of trade more thoughtfully. Companies and governments can—and should—help citizens cope with the faster rate of job change. Together, they should offer retraining and lifelong educational opportunities, wage insurance, and portable health and pension benefits. Doing so would cost only a fraction of the economic benefits that off-shoring will bring.

Little impact on employment and wages

Given that service industries account for nearly 80 percent of employment and virtually all of new job creation in the United States, worries about job losses due to offshoring are understandable. Alarmists claim that nearly all service jobs can be done remotely, owing to advances in technology and telecommunications, and that wages will decline as a result. But the reality is far different.

Pace of offshoring Is evolutionary, not revolutionary

Our research shows that, even theoretically, only 11 percent of all US services jobs could possibly be performed offshore. This is mostly because a large percentage of service jobs—for example, shelf stocking, dental work, medical care, and network installation—require face-to-face customer interactions or a worker's physical presence. In two of the largest sectors in the service economy—health care and retail—only 8 percent and 3 percent of jobs respectively could be performed remotely for this reason. And the industries in which the highest percentage of jobs could be performed remotely—packaged software (49 percent) and IT services (44 percent)—represent only 1 or 2 percent of overall employment ("Portion of jobs that can theoretically go offshore").

Moreover, only a small fraction of the service jobs that could theoretically be performed offshore actually will be. There are several reasons. First, about one-third of U.S. workers are employed by companies with less than 100 employees, and these

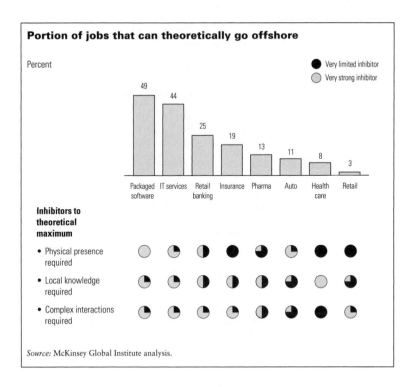

Portion of jobs that can theoretically go offshore

Percent

● Very limited inhibitor
○ Very strong inhibitor

49 — Packaged software
44 — IT services
25 — Retail banking
19 — Insurance
13 — Pharma
11 — Auto
8 — Health care
3 — Retail

Inhibitors to theoretical maximum

- Physical presence required
- Local knowledge required
- Complex interactions required

Source: McKinsey Global Institute analysis.

companies lack sufficient scale to justify the cost involved in off-shoring. For a company with, say, just three to five finance and accounting people, the potential wage savings from moving the tasks to India are too small to justify the management time and effort required.

Even larger companies find offshoring is more complex than they expect. Many would need to put in place a comprehensive package of measures to streamline and adapt their processes and information systems before offshoring could be feasible. The U.S. health care system, for instance, is dominated by paper-based processes that would need to be simplified and digitized; banking and insurance companies would have to integrate their legacy computer systems with those of overseas service providers. Other companies have little global experience and this makes them hesitant to employ people offshore. In fact, our research finds that management resistance is the biggest factor holding back offshoring today, not government regulations.

Furthermore, the rational location for many of the jobs that could, in theory, be performed remotely will *still* be the US. Our research shows that companies consider a host of factors beyond labor cost when deciding where to locate an activity, and then assign different weights to each. These factors include the location's risk profile, the quality of its infrastructure, the size of its domestic market, non-labor costs, its business and living environment, and the availability of vendors.[5] Because of its low-cost, reliable telecommunications and electricity infrastructure, large domestic market, and low political risk, the United States remains the most logical choice for many companies that do not rank cost well above other factors. That's why it attracts so much job-creating investment from foreign companies.

Job loss will be limited

All these factors mean that just a fraction of the jobs that could potentially go offshore actually will. We expect that US companies will create 200,000 to 300,000 offshore jobs per year over the next 30 years. By 2008, our research shows that offshoring will affect less than 2 percent of all service jobs.

It's important to keep in mind that jobs performed in low-wage countries do not necessarily represent jobs lost at home. In fact, many of these jobs would not be viable at higher wage levels. Take E-Telecare, a call-center vendor in the Philippines. It employs one manager for every eight customer service agents, compared with a ratio of 1:20 or more in comparable US call centers. A US airline has found that, because of lower wage levels in India, it can employ additional staff to pursue much smaller delinquent accounts than it could afford to chase before. Another example is the fact that more newspapers are now digitizing back issues, because offshore wages make it economical to do so.

There is a growing body of evidence in addition to our own findings that offshoring will not lead to massive net job losses. The US Bureau of Labor Statistics reports that only 1 percent of service layoffs involving more than 50 employees in the first quarter of 2004 was due to offshoring. A new academic study by Mary Amiti and Shang Jin Wei confirms that, in the United States and the United Kingdom, those service sectors subject to offshoring do not experience net job losses. Put another way, these sectors are creating as many—or more—new jobs than the ones that move offshore.[6]

Imperceptible impact on wages

Because offshoring has such a limited impact on the US jobs market, the effect on wages in the United States will be negligible. This is the case even in the computer and data-processing industry, one of the sectors most affected by offshoring. In the United States, overall employment in that industry has been growing at over 2 percent per year since 2000, compared to 0.4 percent for the rest economy. Although many programming jobs have moved offshore, more positions for systems analysts and software engineers have been created in the United States. And average wages have actually *grown* at a faster pace than elsewhere in the economy, since the new jobs have higher productivity and create more value (see "Shift toward higher-value-added occupations in software and IT services").[7]

Indeed, new research by Brad Jansen and Lori Kletzer finds that service sectors facing international trade competition, such as software publishing and the securities industry, have fared

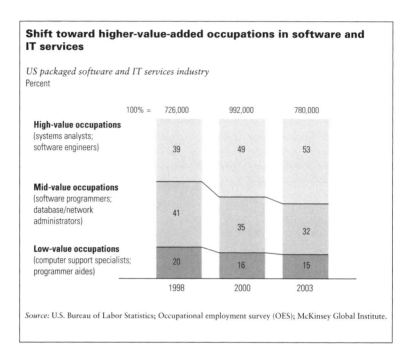

Shift toward higher-value-added occupations in software and IT services

US packaged software and IT services industry
Percent

	726,000	992,000	780,000
High-value occupations (systems analysts; software engineers)	39	49	53
Mid-value occupations (software programmers; database/network administrators)	41	35	32
Low-value occupations (computer support specialists; programmer aides)	20	16	15
	1998	2000	2003

Source: U.S. Bureau of Labor Statistics; Occupational employment survey (OES); McKinsey Global Institute.

better in terms of employment and wages than sectors that don't, such as newspapers and waste management.[8] Between 1999 and 2003, employment grew 7.6 percent per year in tradable services compared to 6.7 percent annually in non-tradable services. Wages are 5 to 10 percent higher in tradable service industries. The authors conclude that exposure to trade in services is consistent with building US competitive advantage.

Why offshoring is good for the United States

Worries about job losses resulting from offshoring have diverted attention from the substantial benefits it generates. Past MGI research found that for every $1 of cost on services that US companies move offshore, at least $1.14 of value is created for the US economy in return.[9] This is, in fact, a conservative estimate since it assumes that only two-thirds of workers find new jobs within six months, as they have historically. But the evidence suggests that the lower cost structure that companies achieve through offshoring results in new business opportunities that, in turn, lead to more jobs being created.

A large part of the benefit of offshoring accrues to companies. For every dollar of cost that US companies move offshore, on average they save 0.58 cents and yet receive largely identical—and sometimes even better—services. This gives them the scope to invest in new technologies and business opportunities that create jobs both at home and abroad, and to distribute some of the savings to shareholders (in the form of higher dividends) and consumers (in the form of lower prices and better quality).

Of arguably even more importance, offshoring enables companies to enhance their competitiveness by taking advantage of distinctive skills abroad.[10] For instance, Chinese wireless chip and software designers, Taiwanese notebook manufacturers, and Philippines call centers have some of the most sophisticated capabilities in the world. By moving its operations to China, one US electronics maker has tripled its manufacturing productivity and, at the same time, cut product development cycle times and defects. In an era of global competition, companies can't afford to pass up on such opportunities.

The United States also benefits from offshoring because it is often on the *receiving* end of jobs and investment. In 2004, the United States received $121 billion of direct investment from foreign companies, the highest in the world.[11] Foreign subsidiaries provided jobs for 5.4 million US workers in 2002—5 percent of all private-sector jobs. They also accounted for 14 percent of US private sector R&D expenditures in 2002, and 20 percent of US exports.[12] Examples of such investment include Novartis opening an R&D lab in Boston, and Philips Electronics moving the headquarters of its global medical systems to Andover, Massachusetts.

With the world's most developed and competitive service industries, the United States stands to benefit more than any other country from free trade in services. It continues to maintain a trade surplus in services, even with India. In 2003, the United States exported $15 billion more business services than it imported.[13] (See "The rest of the world offshores services to the United States and United Kingdom.") US trade negotiators have long argued for freer trade in services, precisely because so many companies in financial services, accounting, law, consulting, and IT services, to name a few, stand to benefit. They should continue to press their case—MGI found that the United States

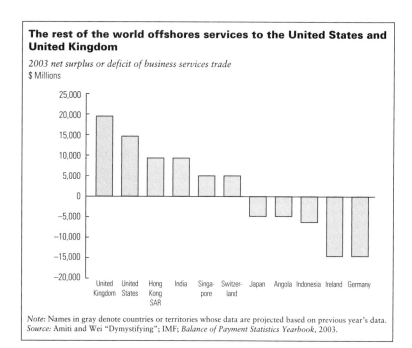

The rest of the world offshores services to the United States and United Kingdom

2003 net surplus or deficit of business services trade
$ Millions

Note: Names in gray denote countries or territories whose data are projected based on previous year's data.
Source: Amiti and Wei "Dymystifying"; IMF; *Balance of Payment Statistics Yearbook,* 2003.

could eliminate up to a third of its current account deficit if countries in the European Union imported as many services from the United States as it imports from them.

Finally, growth in the US workforce will slow in coming years as the baby boomers retire, thus reducing the ratio of workers to retirees. According to figures from the US Census Bureau, US companies will have to make do with 15.6 million fewer workers by 2015. That means they will have to find improvements in productivity, and using offshore labor can be part of the solution—even if only a small part.

Shifting the debate

It is clear that offshoring and openness to trade generate substantial economic benefits. But it is also doubtless the case that a price is being paid in terms of individual job security. Workers face a higher level of job turnover than ever before. Rather than a single career with one or two companies, most workers in the United States and other developed economies today can expect to have jobs with many employers, perhaps even in different fields, and that's a difficult adjustment.

In liberalized, competitive economies with flexible labor markets, there will be plenty of new jobs. According to the OECD, the United States has the world's highest reemployment rate by almost a factor of two. Remaining open to offshoring and inward investment will stimulate more new jobs. Nevertheless, workers need help coping with the accelerated pace of job change that accompanies openness.

Rather than trying to prevent offshoring, governments and companies should therefore turn their attention to designing programs to ease the transition for workers displaced by trade and adjusting education policies to prepare citizens for more flexible careers.

Ease the transition for displaced workers

Historical data show that not all workers who lose their jobs will find new ones quickly and many who do will have to accept pay cuts. A study by J. Bradford Jensen and Lori Kletzer of the University of California Santa Cruz[14] finds that more than 75 percent of service workers who lose their jobs due to trade find new jobs within six months; however, the median wage of those reemployed is 11 percent below their median wage in their previous jobs, reflecting a loss of seniority and experience, and the fact that some switch to new fields.[15]

The United States already has some policies in place to assist workers displaced by trade and other factors, but they are not sufficient. The largest program is unemployment insurance, which absorbs 80 percent of the budget for displaced workers. Full-time, involuntarily displaced workers receive up to 26 weeks of benefits that average around 50 percent of their earnings in their previous jobs. Since the ratification of the Workforce Investment Act of 1998, they have also been offered a set of active reemployment services through one-stop employment centers. These include job search assistance, counseling, and access to training (often through training vouchers).

In addition, the United States has two policies specifically geared to workers displaced by trade: the Trade Adjustment Assistance (TAA) and Alternative Trade Adjustment Assistance programs (ATAA). Two factors motivate special trade adjustment programs: first, they are often used as bargaining tools in

Congressional negotiations on free trade agreements; second, if entire industries are suffering from trade competition, then workers may suffer longer spells of unemployment and more acute wage loss when displaced. The TAA extends unemployment benefits by 52 weeks and offers training supports and health care credits to workers displaced by trade to help them build a skill that will minimize their wage loss. The ATAA provides wage insurance upon reemployment, a relocation allowance, and training credit. Unfortunately, neither the TAA nor the ATAA have lived up to their promise. The TAA training budget has often run short, and TAA recipients averaged 80 weeks of unemployment in 2001–2003, as opposed to 14.1 weeks for all displaced manufacturing workers. Furthermore, their earnings in their new jobs were 21 percent lower, compared with a drop in earnings of 20 percent for all displaced manufacturing workers. The ATAA meanwhile enrolled only 288 participants in 2001–2003.[16]

Spending only 0.5 percent of GDP on all policies to assist displaced workers the United States certainly ranks low in the range of what developed nations allocate to this area—the United Kingdom spends 0.9 percent of GDP, Germany 3.1 percent of GDP, and Denmark 3.7 percent of GDP. Yet the United States has the highest job churn rate among developed countries. Further spending on several policies could do much to ease displaced workers' transition into new employment. For example, job retraining credits given to employers would create an incentive to hire displaced workers. Moreover, on-the-job training has been shown to have an internal rate of return of 10–26 percent, the highest of all forms of training.[17] Continuing education grants give workers a chance to build those skills that are in demand, particularly from growing areas of the economy such as healthcare, education, and social services.[18] These programs are most effective when targeted at skills that have clear job relevance, such as math and science skills.[19] Portable medical insurance plans and pension benefits are also essential to a workforce changing jobs more frequently.

Companies benefiting from offshoring also have a responsibility to displaced workers. Generous severance packages are an obvious way they can help. Companies could also fund wage insurance programs that make up some or all of the difference between workers' previous wages and their new ones, thus encouraging them to get back into the workforce quickly and avoid long-term unemployment. Building on a proposal by Lori Kletzer and Robert Litan,[20] MGI calculated that US companies could make up 70 percent of lost wages for all full-time employees displaced by offshoring, as well as give them healthcare subsidies for up to two years, at a cost of just 4 to 5 percent of their cost savings from offshoring over the same period.

In addition, policy makers might consider extending wage insurance to all displaced workers, whether the cause of their displacement is trade, automation, corporate restructuring, or other factors. Globalization and advances in technology require a more flexible and fluid workforce than ever before and giving companies this flexibility is critical to the national well-being. But there is no reason that individual workers should bear the full cost. Lael Brainard, Robert Litan, and Nicholas Warren recommend a wage insurance that insures 30–70 percent of wage loss for two years for all involuntarily displaced full-time workers with two years or more of tenure. The program would cost only $1.5 billion to $7 billion under the various designs, which amounts to only $12 to $50 per worker per year.[21]

Forward-looking labor unions are already beginning to push for this kind of approach instead of trying to protect existing jobs. For instance, the US IT firm Computer Sciences Corporation (CSC) has struck a deal with the UK union Amicus that it will retrain 10,000 UK staff when it moves their work offshore. Similar deals have been agreed between unions and UK banks.[22] This kind of response to offshoring gives union members a better chance of long-term future employment than struggling to preserve existing jobs at all costs.

Prepare people for more job changes during their working lives

Globalization is producing more frequent and dramatic shifts in companies' demand for labor and it is vital to prepare people to work in such an economy. This will require changes to the US educational system, and a new approach to career changes.

Students will need a broader set of skills beyond technical ones. While IT jobs that require only technical knowledge may well go offshore, those requiring business knowledge, teamwork, and interactions with technology users at home will continue to grow. For example, systems analysts and software engineers in the United States will still be required to set up and customize computer networks for companies, even if computer programmers in India write the software code. (This is why the BLS predicts that employment in computer-related occupations will continue to grow, and why, despite offshoring, it reached a five-year high in the last quarter of 2004.)

Engineering, computer science, and other science programs at US universities must adapt their curricula in response to these shifts and increase the number of courses students take in other disciplines. Understanding how IT can be applied in various fields will be more important than specialist knowledge of particular technology tools. Students will need to combine IT skills with business knowledge, psychology, and anthropology, for instance. In response to shifts in the economy, several US universities are already offering multidisciplinary programs in "services science" that combine insights from engineering, computing, social sciences, and economics and will enable students to develop innovations that will improve productivity in the economy's huge service sectors.

At the same time, industry associations, unions, and companies can combine to help workers anticipate job changes. They can, for example, monitor occupations where employment demand is rising—in healthcare, business services, communications, and leisure—and plot potential career paths for workers switching into them. Software programmers may be required to become systems analysts; radiologists may need to become specialists in treating diabetes.[23] Instead of leaving it to individual workers to spot opportunities and become qualified to grasp them, companies and unions can identify what steps are needed to switch. Continuing education grants and job retraining opportunities are also essential.

Remain attractive to offshoring investment

Although the United States is a world leader in receiving offshoring investment from foreign companies, it still needs to take care to maintain this enviable position and offset those jobs lost to offshoring. Two potential weaknesses are its telecommunication infrastructure and rising health costs. The quality and breadth of US wireless networks lag behind most other developed countries—and even many emerging markets. The United States has fallen to sixteenth in the world in broadband connectivity. At the same time, employee healthcare costs have been rising—by 38 percent between 2001 and 2004—and this is imposing a huge burden on employers.[24] CEOs and other executives regularly mention rising health benefit costs as a factor in their decision to offshore. US policy makers cannot avoid addressing both of these issues if the country is to continue being a magnet for foreign investment.

Fears about job losses and wage cuts in the United States due to offshoring are vastly overstated. Protectionism may save a few jobs in the short-term, but it will stifle innovation and job creation in the longer term. Rather than trying to stop globalization, the goal must be to facilitate and ease the changes it brings.

Is offshoring a harmful form of trade?

In 2004, Nobel Laureate Paul Samuelson published an article reminding readers that, in certain circumstances, free trade can erode the comparative advantage of rich countries and leave them worse off.[a] He presents a theoretical model with two countries (one high-wage, one low-wage), and two goods (one high-value-added and one lower-value-added). He shows that if the low-wage country has a massive workforce that can produce the high-value-added good and if its relative productivity in that good rises, the developed country's terms of trade will deteriorate dramatically and so leave it worse off.

Does this model apply to offshoring today? Our data suggests it does not.[b] First, despite huge populations, low-wage countries don't currently have huge numbers of university graduates *with the skills needed to work for a multinational company* (a proxy for their ability to produce high-value-added goods). Despite having many more college graduates than high-wage countries, on average only 13 percent of them could work for a multinational company. As a result, the number of workers with comparable skills in high-wage countries far outweighs the number in low-wage countries. The United States, for instance, has 10 times the number of skilled workers that China has.

Furthermore, the actual rate has been, and will continue to be, at too low a level to have an adverse impact on a developed country's terms of trade. Indeed, academic researchers have found that, since 1990, the terms of trade for the United States have been stable, or even slightly improved.[c] Finally, our evidence shows that offshoring most often involves relocating the lower-value-added parts of a business process to low-wage countries, not high-value-added services. This reinforces, rather than erodes, the productivity advantage of high-wage countries.

So even in a two-good, two-country model of trade, the implication that offshoring is a harmful form of trade is not supported by our data. Furthermore, in the real world, countries trade not just two but many services, creating even more opportunities to specialize and develop a comparative advantage.

---

a. Paul Samuelson, "Where Ricardo and Mill rebut and confirm arguments of mainstream economists supporting globalization," *Journal of Economic Perspectives,* Vol. 18, No. 3, Summer 2004, pp. 135–146.

b. Other economists agree. See Jagdish Bhagwatl, Arvind Panagariya, and T. N. Srinivasan, "The muddles over outsourcing," *Journal of Economic Perspectives,* Vol. 18, No. 4, Fall 2004, pp. 93–414.

c. See Avinash Dixit and Gene Grossman, "Samuelson says nothing about trade policy," commentary posted on Avinash Dixit's personal home page at www .princeton.edu/dlxitak/home/CommentOnSamuelson.pdf.

McKinsey Global Institute, October, 2005.

Notes

1. Daniel Yankelovich, "Poll positions," *Foreign Affairs*, September/October 2005.

2. See "The emerging global labor market" available for free at www.mckinsey.com/mgi, or Diana Farrell, Martha A. Laboissière, and Jaeson Rosenfeld, "Sizing the emerging global labor market," *The McKinsey Quarterly*, 2005 number 3.

3. This figure is for gross job gains. Subtracting job losses, there were 2.09 million net new jobs created. Source: Bureau of Labor Statistics.

4. Nobel Laureate Paul Samuelson has argued that offshoring will not benefit the home economy if the terms of trade for a nation change enough. Our research shows this is unlikely to be the case, however. See "Is offshoring a harmful form of trade?" for more.

5. We created a Location Cost Index (LCI) database that captures data on over 50 factors that companies use when deciding where to locate an activity.

6. Mary Amiti and Shang-Jin Wei, "Demystifying outsourcing: the numbers do not support the hype over job losses," *Finance & Development*, December 2004.

7. In the United Kingdom, employment in the sector grew at 6.6 percent per year from 1998–2004, while employment decreased by 1.8 percent per year across all occupations. Wages in the sector grew slightly less fast than overall wages, however.

8. J. Bradford Jensen and Lori G. Kletzer, "Tradeable services: understanding the scope and impact of services offshoring," working paper, July 14, 2005.

9. See Martin N. Baily and Diana Farrell, "Exploding the myths of offshoring," *The McKinsey Quarterly*, available online at www.mckinseyquarterly.com.

10. John Hagel III, "Offshoring goes on the offensive," *The McKinsey Quarterly*, 2004 number 2.

11. Source: UNCTAD.

12. Data is from the US Bureau of Economic Analysis; 2002 is the latest available. See Matthew J. Slaughter, "Insourcing Jobs: Making the Global Economy Work for America," Dartmouth University, October 2004.

13. Amiti and Wei, "Demystifying Outsourcing."

14. Jensen and Kletzer, "Tradable services."

15. But even at this level of re-employment and new wages, MGI found that offshoring generates a net benefit for the US economy. See Vivek Agrawal and Diana Farrell, "Who wins in offshoring?" *The McKinsey Quarterly*, 2003 special edition: *Global directions*.

16. Many of the statistics on the TAA and ATAA are from Lael Brainard, Robert Litan, and Nicholas Warren "Insuring America's Workers in a New Era of Offshoring," Brookings Institute Policy Brief 143, Washington DC, July 2005.

17. Lisa M. Lynch, ed. *Training and the Private Sector: International Comparison* (Chicago: University of Chicago Press 1994).

18. Frank Levy and Richard Munrane, *How Computers are Creating the Next Job Market*. Princeton University Press, Princeton, NJ, 2004.

19. Lisa M. Lynch, "Job Loss: Bridging the Research and Policy Discussion," IZA Discussion Paper No. 1518, 2005.

20. Lori Kletzer and Robert Litan, "A prescription to relieve worker anxiety," Policy Brief 01–2, Institute for International Economics, February 2001.

21. Brainard, Litan, and Warren, "Insuring America's Workers in a New Era of Offshoring."

22. Andrew Taylor, "IT group agrees landmark jobs deal with union," *Financial Times*, August 9, 2005.

23. Jagdish Baghwati, "A new vocabulary for trade," *Wall Street Journal*, August 4, 2005.

24. David Wessel, "Capital: Healthcare costs blamed for hiring gap," *Wall Street Journal*, March 11, 2004.

9

How France and Germany can benefit from offshoring

IDEAS IN BRIEF

Offshoring in France and Germany, unlike in the United States, does not currently return a net gain to their economies.

Despite having fewer low-wage locations to choose from because of their language requirements, French and German companies can save costs, as well as freedom from market barriers at home that stifle innovation, by offshoring.

However, reemploying workers displaced by offshoring remains a challenge for these economies, especially Germany. More flexible labor polices would offer a remedy.

France and Germany could turn their net losses from offshoring into gains if they undertook the structural economic reforms that both countries need.

German and French companies benefit from offshoring service jobs to low-wage countries. Yet neither Germany nor France makes a net financial gain as a result. However, this is a symptom of underlying economic problems that both countries need to tackle, not a signal to curb offshoring.

A recent survey[1] shows that 40 percent of western Europe's 500 largest companies have begun moving their service operations abroad. This should be good news for the region's economy. Research by the McKinsey Global Institute (MGI) shows offshoring service jobs can create wealth both for the economy that exports jobs and for the one that receives them.[2]

However, offshoring does neither for France and Germany at the moment. MGI has found that every euro of corporate spending that French and German companies send offshore returns just €0.86 of value for France's economy, and only €0.80 for Germany's. Yet the US economy gains roughly $1.15 in new wealth for every dollar of corporate spending that US companies outsource abroad, making offshoring a win-win game (see "Economic impact of offshoring of services in the United States, Germany, and France).

White-collar workers in France and Germany, formerly shielded from global competition, are anxious that offshoring could lose them their jobs. Policy makers in both countries are understandably minded to curb the practice. But its negative effects are symptomatic of deeper economic issues that deserve their entire attention.

Sluggish GDP and employment growth ail both economies. To achieve faster growth and create more jobs, policy makers need to reduce any product market barriers stifling competition and

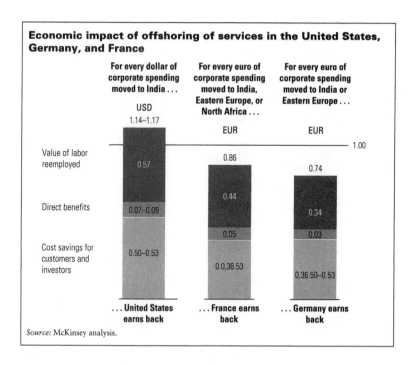

Economic impact of offshoring of services in the United States, Germany, and France

	For every dollar of corporate spending moved to India ... USD 1.14–1.17	For every euro of corporate spending moved to India, Eastern Europe, or North Africa ... EUR	For every euro of corporate spending moved to India or Eastern Europe ... EUR
			1.00
Value of labor reemployed	0.57	0.86	0.74
Direct benefits	0.07–0.09	0.44	0.34
		0.05	0.03
Cost savings for customers and investors	0.50–0.53	0.0,36.53	0,36.50–0.53
	... United States earns back	... France earns back	... Germany earns back

Source: McKinsey analysis.

innovation, and introduce more flexible labor policies. One outcome of these measures will be a higher rate of reemployment for displaced workers. And with a higher reemployment rate, the economies of both countries will turn their losses from offshoring into net financial gains.

Offshoring is a powerful way for companies to reduce their costs, improve the quality of their offerings, and remain competitive in global markets. For these reasons, while governments can and should help ease the plight of any workers displaced through offshoring, curbing offshoring itself would be the wrong way for French and German policy makers to respond to the problems it raises. On the contrary, they should leave companies free to pursue offshoring opportunities and concentrate on delivering the structural economic reforms that both countries need. Success in this endeavor will automatically turn offshoring from a burden into a benefit for both their economies.

The economic impact of offshoring

In August 2003 the McKinsey Global Institute published an analysis of the economic benefits, both direct and indirect, of offshoring back-office service and IT functions from the United States to India.[3] Of the direct benefits, MGI found that every dollar of spending that US companies transfer to India creates as much as $1.46 in new wealth globally. Of this, India receives 33 cents, through wages paid to local workers, profits earned by Indian outsourcing providers and their suppliers, and additional taxes collected by the government. The US economy captures the remaining $1.13 through cost savings to businesses, increased exports to India, repatriated earnings from offshore providers in which US companies have invested, and the additional economic output created when US workers are re-employed in other jobs.

But a similar analysis shows that Germany captures just €0.80 for every euro of corporate spending on service functions moved offshore, and France only €0.86. To understand these gaps, consider how offshoring creates wealth for an economy (see "Benefits of offshoring for French, German, or US economies").

Cost savings for companies

In the United States, companies save 58 cents for every dollar of spending on back-office service functions and IT jobs they move to India. These savings can then be reinvested in new business opportunities with higher value added, passed on to consumers in the form of lower prices (which then spark growth in demand), or distributed to shareholders.

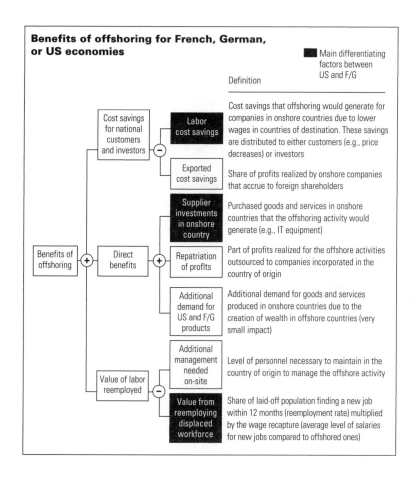

Benefits of offshoring for French, German, or US economies

Main differentiating factors between US and F/G

		Definition
Labor cost savings		Cost savings that offshoring would generate for companies in onshore countries due to lower wages in countries of destination. These savings are distributed to either customers (e.g., price decreases) or investors
Exported cost savings		Share of profits realized by onshore companies that accrue to foreign shareholders
Supplier investments in onshore country		Purchased goods and services in onshore countries that the offshoring activity would generate (e.g., IT equipment)
Repatriation of profits		Part of profits realized for the offshore activities outsourced to companies incorporated in the country of origin
Additional demand for US and F/G products		Additional demand for goods and services produced in onshore countries due to the creation of wealth in offshore countries (very small impact)
Additional management needed on-site		Level of personnel necessary to maintain in the country of origin to manage the offshore activity
Value from reemploying displaced workforce		Share of laid-off population finding a new job within 12 months (reemployment rate) multiplied by the wage recapture (average level of salaries for new jobs compared to offshored ones)

German companies save only €0.52 for every euro of corporate spending on jobs they offshore to India, because differences in language and culture make it more expensive to coordinate such offshoring projects. For those reasons, German companies send the majority of their offshore work to Eastern Europe. But here, they save still less.[4] Wages and infrastructure costs are higher in Eastern Europe, a disadvantage only partially offset by lower telecommunications expenses, lower margins for Eastern European outsourcing providers, and lower tax rates.[5] Averaging the savings across both India and Eastern Europe, German companies save €0.48 for every euro of spending they send offshore.

The French companies engaged in offshoring save even less. They tend to locate offshore jobs not in India but in central Europe and North Africa, where fluent French speakers are more plentiful but wages are higher. As a result, they get back only €0.36 in costs saved from every euro spent offshore (see "Labor costs in offshoring locations").

Added flexibility for companies

In a single respect—added flexibility for companies in deploying labor and responding to shifts in demand—offshoring helps

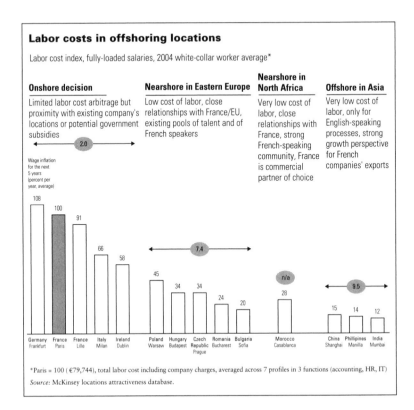

Labor costs in offshoring locations

Labor cost index, fully-loaded salaries, 2004 white-collar worker average*

Onshore decision	Nearshore in Eastern Europe	Nearshore in North Africa	Offshore in Asia
Limited labor cost arbitrage but proximity with existing company's locations or potential government subsidies	Low cost of labor, close relationships with France/EU, existing pools of talent and of French speakers	Very low cost of labor, close relationships with France, strong French-speaking community, France is commercial partner of choice	Very low cost of labor, only for English-speaking processes, strong growth perspective for French companies' exports

Wage inflation for the next 5 years (percent per year, average)

Onshore decision: 2.0
Nearshore in Eastern Europe: 7.4
Nearshore in North Africa: n/a
Offshore in Asia: 9.5

Germany Frankfurt	France Paris	France Lille	Italy Milan	Ireland Dublin	Poland Warsaw	Hungary Budapest	Czech Republic Prague	Romania Bucharest	Bulgaria Sofia	Morocco Casablanca	China Shanghai	Phillipines Manila	India Mumbai
108	100	91	66	58	45	34	34	24	20	28	15	14	12

*Paris = 100 (€79,744), total labor cost including company charges, averaged across 7 profiles in 3 functions (accounting, HR, IT).

Source: McKinsey locations attractiveness database.

German companies more than their US counterparts, and the same is likely to be true for French companies. Strict German laws about laying off workers and creating new job categories mean that German companies have more trouble adjusting their use of labor than US ones do. As a result, the Germans are more likely to face poor utilization rates and problems adusting their labor force to match changing market circumstances. The use of foreign labor gives these companies more flexibility to experiment with new ideas and respond to market changes. Although we can't quantify the magnitude of this benefit, interviews with German and other European CEOs suggest that it can be substantial for many companies. German and French companies may gain from offshoring a greater increase in control over their use of labor than do companies based in the United States, where labor regulations are less restrictive to start with.

New revenues for the economy

Offshoring can boost a country's export earnings as well, thereby generating economic wealth. The outsourcing providers— whether they do business in India or in Poland, and whether they are subsidiaries of multinational companies or independently owned businesses—buy many goods and services abroad. A call center in Bangalore, for instance, might purchase Dell computers, HP printers, Microsoft software, and Siemens telephones. MGI estimates that for every dollar of US corporate spending that moves to India, US exports there increase by five cents. This statistic partly explains why exports from the United States to India grew from $3.7 billion in 2000 to $5 billion in 2003.

For European economies, the increase in high-tech exports is somewhat smaller, mainly because US companies dominate the sector. For every euro of spending on work outsourced to India or eastern Europe from Germany, for example, MGI estimates that it gains €0.03 from new exports. The benefit to France is roughly the same.

Offshoring can also boost repatriated earnings when domestic companies own stakes in offshore ventures, as they often do. Indian firms wholly or partly owned by US companies generate 30 percent of the revenues of the Indian IT-outsourcing and business-process outsourcing industries. An additional four cents of every dollar spent on offshoring services to India thus returns to the United States in the form of repatriated profits. German companies, however, hold only negligible positions in eastern European and Indian outsourcing providers and thus miss out on this revenue. French companies do a little better from this source, but France gains a total of only €0.05 from increased exports to offshore locations and repatriated profits from offshore providers combined (compared with 9 cents for the United States).

Value from redeploying workers

In the United States, many people whose work is outsourced move on to other, higher-value-added activities. From 1979 to 1999, 69 percent of US workers who lost their jobs as a result of trade in sectors other than manufacturing found new work within half a year.[6] On average, they received similar wages in their new jobs (though roughly half took pay cuts).

For each dollar of work offshored, the US economy gains 57 cents from the rapid reemployment of laid-off workers in higher-value-adding jobs. But France gains only €0.44 and Germany only €0.34 in this way, because their less flexible labor markets and lower levels of job creation mean that fewer workers find new employment quickly. This is largely why offshoring is, at present, a net drain on both their economies.

In Germany, only 39 percent of laid-off workers find new jobs within a year, compared with the United States' 69 percent. Some 4.3 million Germans are unemployed, partly as a result of the integration of East Germany into the German Federal Republic, and job growth is very slow. But if Germany could increase its reemployment rate to match that of the United States, offshoring would create €1.05 of value for the German economy for every euro offshored.

About 60 percent of laid-off French workers find new jobs within a year, we estimate. But France, too, has a high level of unemployment and a labor policy framework that makes it difficult to create new jobs. As in Germany, raising the reemployment rate of the workers affected by offshoring is the key challenge for French policy makers and businesses.

The route to reform

Companies that embrace offshoring early in the game will earn surpluses that enable them to create new jobs, both at home and abroad. Those resisting the trend will find themselves at a cost disadvantage that will increasingly erode their market share and eventually destroy jobs at home. For these reasons, it would be a mistake spend time and effort legislating against offshoring.

Instead, policy makers in Germany and France should remain focused on creating new momentum in their economies and more flexibility in their labor markets. By doing so, both countries can ensure they remain competitive in the global economy, and generate the GDP and employment growth both seek. Moreover, in a dynamic, competitive economy, displaced workers will be rapidly reemployed, ensuring a positive return to the economy from offshoring.

The challenges facing Germany

Since 1993, employment in Germany has increased by only 0.2 percent a year, compared with 1.2 percent in the rest of the European Union, and economic growth has averaged just 1.4 percent a year, little more than half the average for the rest of the European Union and far below the US growth rate of 3.3 percent. A variety of market restrictions—price regulations, zoning laws, subsidies—hold back growth by distorting and dampening competition and innovation.

Limits on the operating hours of stores, for instance, prevent retailers from realizing the better service and higher employment that would come from remaining open longer. In the automotive, retail trade, road freight, and utilities sectors, regulatory barriers directly or indirectly limit market access, and competition and innovation are therefore much less common than they are in comparable countries without such barriers. In retail banking, small state-owned and cooperative banks with sub-scale operations and little shareholder pressure prevent consolidation and dampen competition.

To get the full value of offshoring, Germany needs to create more jobs in high-value-added occupations. That means revising any inappropriate product market regulations that stifle competition and innovation. Without pressure from competitors, companies have little incentive to innovate and boost productivity on an ongoing basis. Although some people might think that higher productivity means fewer jobs, the empirical evidence shows that it will actually generate economic growth immediately as well as employment in the long run, in mature, advanced economies such as Germany, France and the United States.[7] Higher productivity lets the companies that achieve it offer consumers lower prices and better value, thus stimulating demand and allowing more productive competitors to take market share from less productive ones.

To speed up the transition from today's jobs to tomorrow's, German policy makers need to make labor markets more flexible as well. High wages have contributed to the lackluster growth in jobs. Although Germany doesn't have a minimum wage, the combined impact of wage floors set through collective bargaining and social benefits for the long-term jobless create an effective minimum employment cost, making many lower-paid jobs economically unfeasible. The creation of "minijobs" that pay €400 to €800 a month for part-time work was meant to tackle this problem, but research has shown that they have mainly cannibalized full-time jobs rather than created new ones.[8]

German businesses are also cautious about adding new workers because of the need to get approval from worker representatives. Companies must often wait six months or longer to hire new workers, and using temporary ones involves extensive mandatory paperwork. The procedures for laying off workers are equally burdensome. For one multinational German company, a recent round of layoffs took two weeks to accomplish in the United States, four weeks in the United Kingdom, and three months in Germany.[9]

In addition, Germany would benefit from adapting its education systems to reflect the needs of a changing labor market more closely. The offshoring of IT jobs may well aggravate overcapacity in the youth job market, for example. But IT engineers can be trained to undertake higher-value, less commoditized activities that are less vulnerable to offshoring. A study of the US labor market from 1999 to 2003[10] suggests that although offshoring probably reduced demand for lower-end computer programmers, the number of software engineers and network systems analysts working on higher-end activities actually increased greatly over the same time period.

Boosting innovation and job creation in France

Offshoring has so far had a negligible impact in France. Between 2002 and 2004, moving jobs offshore accounted for only 4 percent of the total number of jobs lost—and the majority of these were in manufacturing. But as global competition heats up, French companies are likely to follow their US and UK competitors offshore in search of cost savings.

To capture the full economic benefit from offshoring, France must first capture more of the potential cost savings offshoring can offer. The mix of offshoring destinations changes the net economic impact of offshoring in the home country significantly. French companies need French-speaking workers, which limits their choice of offshore locations. But they still have a choice: offshoring to North Africa generates potentially more cost savings than to some eastern Europe destinations. Integrating offshoring in the Euromed initiative, which would create a free trade area between the EU, Mediterranean, and North African countries, could help North African countries build the necessary infrastructure and vendor base to create a credible alternative to India. This would encourage companies to offshore to North Africa and ultimately benefit French consumers and investors.

Policy makers must also speed the reemployment of French workers displaced by offshoring. As in Germany, this will depend on how successful they are in spurring innovation and creating higher-value-added jobs, while also increasing labor market flexibility. To stimulate innovation, France's government needs to create the conditions for more intense competition between companies. In a 2002 study, MGI compared the performance of six industries in France, Germany, and the United States.[11] We found that France could significantly raise its productivity and employment through the better diffusion of innovations, if the government ensured strong and fair competition and corrected market distortions. To boost competitive intensity in all sectors of the French economy, the government would need to open them further to foreign companies, particularly those from outside Europe, and adjust the many product market, zoning, and labor laws that hinder competition.

To create more jobs, France should look to its domestic service sectors. Services account for 70 percent of total employment across the European Union and for nearly all net new jobs, so they have the greatest potential for creating the largest number of new, high-value-added positions. Employment in sectors such as social services, retailing, and tourism, which could provide millions of new jobs that can't be offshored, is lower in France than in other Western economies.[12]

In France, as in Germany, a raft of regulations on working hours, minimum wages, and the hiring and firing of workers combine to make companies reluctant to hire new staff. France's comparatively generous minimum wage, for instance, has led the retailing industry to rely more on automation and less on labor. As a result French retailers employ half as many workers as their US counterparts, in proportion to the country's population. The way to create a more flexible labor market is to modernize social and employment regulation.

Employment regulations and minimum wages have the critically important social objective of protecting workers. But this can be achieved better by mechanisms that encourage rather than discourage employment, such as financial incentives for unemployed people who return to work or for companies that hire them. In addition, policy makers can target specific categories of employees who lose their job to offshoring for special help in finding another one.

Since workers in the back offices of retail banks, for example, tend to be relatively old, unskilled, and female—all factors that decrease the reemployment rate—many will likely have difficulty finding new work. Policy makers who understand the profiles of the people and occupations most affected (software programmers, call-center agents, back-office service workers) should be able to develop specific programs to raise the reemployment rate and reduce the social impact of offshoring. These could include government job-retraining efforts, incentives for companies to hire and retrain displaced workers, relocation help, and company-sponsored insurance programs, transferable from one employer to another, that would offset wage losses. Such reemployment assistance will not only make economies more flexible and resilient but also reassure frightened workers and reduce political strains.

Sluggish GDP and employment growth are arguably the most important economic issues facing French and German policy makers today. They should not let anxieties aroused by offshoring divert them from their main task: stimulating more competition and innovation between firms, and making their labor markets significantly more flexible. Success will have the added bonus of transforming offshoring into an opportunity for their economies as a whole, rather than only for the firms doing the offshoring.

Tony Blanco, Diana Farrell, and Eric Labaye
The McKinsey Quarterly, Web exclusive, August 2005

Diana Farrell
The McKinsey Quarterly, 2004 Number 4.

Notes

1. "Outsourcing takes off in Europe in a major way," *Straits Times*, June 21, 2004.

2. See Vivek Agrawal and Diana Farrell, "Who wins in off-shoring," *The McKinsey Quarterly*, 2003 special edition: *Global directions*.

3. Vivek Agrawal and Diana Farrell, "Offshoring: Is it a win-win game?," McKinsey Global Institute Perspective, August 2004. Available online at www.mckinsey.com/mgi.

4. Because eastern European countries import more from Germany than India does, the overall value to the German economy is slightly higher.

5. A recent survey of German business executives found that 59 percent of planned offshoring investments were headed for eastern Europe. FTE, August 26, 2003.

6. Lori G. Kletzer and Robert E. Litan, "A prescription to relieve worker anxiety," Policy Brief 01-2, Institute for International Economics, Washington DC, February 2001 (www.iie.com).

7. In developing countries, economic growth is sometimes fueled by increasing the amount of capital used. But once optimal levels of capital intensity are achieved, as they have been in advanced economies, this avenue for growth is closed.

8. Viktor Steiner and Katharina Wrohlich, "Work Incentives and Labor Supply Effects of the 'Minijobs Reform' in Germany," The German Institute for Economic Research, (DIW Berlin), February 27, 2004.

9. *The Economist*, "How to pep up Germany's economy," May 8, 2004.

10. M. Baily and R. Lawrence, "Don't blame trade for US job losses," *McKinsey Quarterly*, 2005 Number 1 (www.mckinseyquarterly.com).

11. "Reaching Higher Productivity Growth in France and Germany," McKinsey Global Institute, 2002 (www.mckinsey.com/mgi).

12. See the Camdessus Report "Le Sursault, vers une nouvelle croissance pour la France," La Documentation Française, 2004.

10

Governing globalization

Diana Farrell

Offshore outsourcing of jobs continues to attract censure, especially in developed countries. Its most vociferous opponents contend that corporations betray their employees by shipping work overseas. Yet research shows that, on the whole, the economies of developed countries benefit from this phenomenon.[1] So do those of developing countries, where new jobs alleviate poverty, improve general living standards, and provide the means to address health and environmental challenges.

In reality, the process of global economic integration—of which offshore outsourcing is a highly visible component—diffuses the best business ideas and management tools, intensifies competition, and sparks innovation. It thereby leads to lower prices and higher wages as well as bigger profits that companies can reinvest in new business opportunities.

Of course, the fact that economic integration benefits the global economy as a whole doesn't mean that it benefits all workers and companies. On the contrary, offshoring can destroy the jobs of workers in developed economies, and incumbent companies in developing ones can lose out to more efficient foreign competitors during the transition to modern production methods. Those hardest hit can face major dislocations and a loss of status.

But understandable as the protectionist reaction to these hardships might be, it is misguided, since it would forestall not only the problems but also the benefits of offshoring. Less understandable, perhaps, is the failure of corporations and governments to do more to ease the suffering of its victims. Companies and policy makers together have the power and the responsibility to help workers deal more flexibly and painlessly with employment changes.

In healthy economies, companies create new jobs—often with higher wages and higher value added to the economy—for most of the people who lose their old ones. Companies can make it easier for their workers to adjust by committing themselves to continual on-the-job learning and retraining programs. Policy makers can assist them by offering tax credits or other incentives for companies that hire and train displaced workers. Generous severance and relocation packages can help as well. So too can wage insurance (see "Easing the pain for workers," in chapter 4 "Who wins in offshoring?").

The loss of employment isn't the only problem. In the United States, when people lose their jobs, a large part of the stress they undergo stems from the loss of pensions and healthcare coverage. A broader commitment by companies and policy makers, working together to increase the portability of healthcare and pension plans would go a long way to ease the transition for people coping with change.

By making any country's labor force more flexible, these policies would allow global economic integration and wealth creation to proceed more smoothly. Protectionism, in contrast, may save a few jobs in the short run, but it stifles innovation and job creation in the long run. Facilitating rather than stopping change must be the goal. To reach it, the public and private sectors will have to collaborate closely.

Diana Farrell,
McKinsey Quarterly, 2004 Number 3.

Index

communications technology, 2
Communications Workers of
America, 58
company-specific considerations,
13
competition
for available talent, 47–49
effects on productivity, 71–72,
125
interference from informal
economy, 81–82
competitive markets. *See also*
emerging markets
FDI and, 80–82
competitiveness, 121, 131, 155,
156
competitive pressure, 36–37,
129–130, 152–153
concentration of demand
alternative solutions, 18–21
in certain locations, 17–18
company objectives and, 18
consumer electronics sector
in China, 74, 81, 97
globalization of, 96–97
local-content requirements, 78,
79
continuing education grants, 135,
138
conversational skills, 53
cost savings
choice of offshore location and,
118, 120, 128
from offshoring, 61, 87,
94–96, 146–148, 154
telecom costs, 93
"crowding in," 78–79

cultural fit, of job candidates, 14,
29–30, 48, 49
customer service centers, 95
Czech Republic, 17, 18, 106, 111

data collection, in comparing
locations, 121
decision criteria, in site selection,
120
demand for offshore labor
in China, 47–49
concentration of demand, 17–21
from developed countries,
11–13, 100
dispersing, 23
effect on employment, 9
implications of, 2–3
in India and Russia, 104
supply inefficiently matched,
11, 17
wages and, 9, 11, 22–24
demand-side countries
effects of offshoring on
employment in, 24
size of global labor market
and, 18–21
developed countries
effects of offshoring on, 9, 159
increasing demand in, 11–13,
100
university graduates in,
108–109
developing nations. *See also* foreign direct investment (FDI)
effects of offshoring on,
159–160

About the Authors

Sizing the emerging global labor market

Diana Farrell is the director of the McKinsey Global Institute, where **Martha A. Laboissière** is a senior fellow, and **Jaeson Rosenfeld** is an MGI external fellow.

Ensuring India's offshoring future

Diana Farrell is the director of the McKinsey Global Institute, **Noshir Kaka** is a principal in McKinsey's Mumbai office, and **Sascha Stürze** is an alumnus from McKinsey's Berlin office and MGI.

China's looming talent shortage

Diana Farrell is the director of the McKinsey Global Institute, and **Andrew Grant** is a director in McKinsey's Shanghai office.

Who wins in offshoring?

Vivek Agrawal is a consultant in McKinsey's Minneapolis office, **Diana Farrell** is the director of the McKinsey Global Institute.

The truth about foreign direct investment in emerging markets

Diana Farrell is the director of the McKinsey Global Institute, where **Jaana Remes** is a senior fellow. **Heiner Schulz** is an alumnus from McKinsey's San Francisco office and MGI.

Offshoring and beyond

Vivek Agrawal is a consultant in McKinsey's Minneapolis office; **Diana Farrell** is the director of the McKinsey Global Institute, where **Jaana Remes** is a senior fellow.

Smarter offshoring

Diana Farrell is the director of the McKinsey Global Institute.

US offshoring: rethinking the response

Diana Farrell is the director of the McKinsey Global Institute. **Jaeson Rosenfeld** is an external fellow.

How France and Germany can benefit from offshoring

Diana Farrell is the director of the McKinsey Global Institute.

Governing globalization

Diana Farrell is the director of the McKinsey Global Institute.